To Maria
With Much Love,
For your birthday —

April 17, 2002

John Millington Synge

Revised Edition

Twayne's English Authors Series

Kinley E. Roby, Editor

Northeastern University

TEAS 12

JOHN MILLINGTON SYNGE
Courtesy of Dublin College

John Millington Synge

Revised Edition

By Donna Gerstenberger

University of Washington

Twayne Publishers
A Division of G. K. Hall & Co. • *Boston*

John Millington Synge, Revised Edition
Donna Gerstenberger

Copyright 1990 by G. K. Hall & Co.
All rights reserved.
Published by Twayne Publishers
A Division of G. K. Hall & Co.
70 Lincoln Street
Boston, Massachusetts 02111

First Edition copyright © 1965 by Twayne Publishers, Inc.

Copyediting supervised by Barbara Sutton
Book production by Gabrielle B. McDonald
Book design by Barbara Anderson

Typeset in 11 pt. Garamond
by Compset, Inc., Beverly, MA

Printed on permanent/durable acid-free paper
and bound in the United States of America

First published 1990.
10 9 8 7 6 5 4 3 2 1

Library of Congress Cataloging-in-Publication Data

Gerstenberger, Donna Lorine.
    John Millington Synge / by Donna Gerstenberger.—Rev. ed.
        p.   cm.—(Twayne's English authors series ; TEAS 12)
    Includes bibliographical references.
    Includes index.
    ISBN 0-8057-6959-5
    1. Synge, J. M. (John Millington), 1871–1909—Criticism and interpretation.
    I. Title.   II. Series.
PR5534.G4   1990
822'.912—dc20   89-38330
                                                              CIP

Contents

About the Author

Donna Gerstenberger is a professor of English at the University of Washington. Her interests are contemporary Irish, American, and English literature. She has published articles and books on Iris Murdoch, W. B. Yeats, and John Millington Synge as well as on modern English and American poetry, fiction, and drama. She is a member of the American Committee for Irish Studies and the American Committee for Irish Studies/West and regularly teaches graduate and undergraduate classes on the Irish renaissance and the Irish Theater movement.

Preface

Not until more than fifty years since his death has John Millington Synge begun to receive the sustained critical attention due him as one of the important figures of Ireland's literary renaissance and as the creator of at least two plays that have become a part of the canon of modern drama. Until 1960 much of Synge's work was out of print or hard to obtain, and only in 1959—fifty years after his death—was the official biography published, the first written with the benefit of all the information available from Synge's own unpublished documents. Before this period critical attention had been sporadic and scarce, and during those years Synge's work often received its best, if incidental, treatment in books about W. B. Yeats in examinations of the relationship of the two contemporaries.

In 1962 the task of making Synge's canon available in a definitive edition was begun with the first of four volumes published by Oxford University Press, an undertaking completed in 1968. The importance of having all of Synge's work available in a scholarly edition cannot be underestimated, for this edition not only brings together published material difficult to locate, it also provides the texts of manuscript work never before published, such as the text of Synge's first completed play, *When the Moon Has Set*. Most important, it serves as a kind of variorum, providing variant versions of the work so that we can better understand Synge as a working artist. Thus the scholar now can trace the transformation of the versions of plays such as *The Playboy of the Western World*. The publication of the collected works not only responded to a growing interest in Synge's work in the 1950s and 1960s, it, in turn, has undoubtedly contributed to an increased attention to Synge's contribution to the Irish renaissance and to the development of modern drama. Second only in importance to the publication of the collected works has been the careful study given in recent years to Synge's language, the most important of these being Declan Kiberd's *Synge and the Irish Language*.

My revised edition of *John Millington Synge* seeks to take account of the various and helpful contributions to our understanding of Synge's work since 1964 and continues the task identified in the first version: to evaluate what is permanent in Synge's accomplishment and to trace where possible the growth of the dramatist. Much past attention to Synge took the form of biographical or historical interest—that is, the *Playboy* riots, his relationship to Lady Gregory and W. B. Yeats—and although this interest continues, important recent critical work has found intellectually interesting contexts for readings of Synge's work, and the redirection of critical interest this book called for in 1964 is an accomplished and welcome fact. The revised *John Millington Synge* takes into account the major work done in recent years and presents the pertinent facts necessary to understand Synge in various contexts, including the historical, but mainly it addresses itself to ways of reading Synge's work with the hope of further widening his audience.

To present all of Synge's production in its most meaningful sequence, the two long prose pieces—*The Aran Islands* and *In Wicklow, West Kerry, and Connemara*—are examined first. These are followed by a chapter on each of the plays, generally in order of creation, with the poems and translations being treated separately. Historical data are given where they seem most likely to illuminate the material under discussion, and critical issues, such as Synge's theories of tragedy and of comedy, are not given treatment in separate chapters. They are, instead, included with specific discussions of the actual practice of tragedy or comedy in the individual plays. The intent of such an organization is that a complete sense of Synge as a working artist may emerge. It is in service of this intention that no attempt has been made to pursue a "thematic" reading of Synge throughout, for although such procedure is tempting for the (often spurious) unity it provides, the thematic patterns that do emerge come out of the work as the result of a growth of art and artist in discovery and technique. They exist as the result of a recurrent and established attitude toward reality.

My acknowledgments are the same, although some of the people who helped me with the original study are no longer living. I wish to express my gratitude to the University of Washington for a leave that enabled me to visit Ireland and to complete this work; to the American Philosophical Society for a grant in support of research; to Professor David H. Greene, Synge's official biographer, for answering my questions; to Professor Roger McHugh, for his kindness during my stay in Dublin; to Elizabeth Dallas for research assistance; to my colleague, Professor Malcolm Brown, for providing books and information; to Carolyn and Gregory Allen for sharing their roof with me while part of this study was being completed; to Lane Fichtenau and the University of Washington Library.

Acknowledgment is also due to Random House, Inc., for permission to reprint passages from *The Complete Works of John M. Synge,* copyright 1935 by Modern Library, Inc.; to Dolmen Press and Thomas Kinsella for permission to quote the last stanza of "Queens" by Thomas Kinsella; to Macmillan and to David H. Greene for permission to use passages from the Greene and Stephens biography, *J. M. Synge,* © 1959 by David H. Greene.

Donna Gerstenberger

University of Washington

Chronology

folklore. First operation for Hodgkin's disease. Friendship with Stephen MacKenna.

1898   Makes first of five visits to the Aran Islands.

1899   Founding of Irish Literary Theatre with productions in the Antient Concert Rooms, Dublin, of Yeats's *The Countess Cathleen* and Edward Martyn's *The Heather Field*.

1902   Decides to abandon Paris for Dublin. Begins active role in the Irish National Theatre Society.

1903   *The Shadow of the Glen* performed in Dublin. *When the Moon Has Set* rejected by W. B. Yeats and Lady Gregory.

1904   First performance of *Riders to the Sea* at Molesworth Hall. Founding of the Abbey Theatre. Publication of *The Shadow of the Glen*.

1905   Production of *The Well of the Saints* at the Abbey Theatre. Makes trip with Jack Yeats through the Congested Districts. Beginning of continental reputation. Travels in Kerry. Membership on Abbey Theatre Board of Directors. First publication of *Riders to the Sea* and of *The Well of the Saints*.

1906   Engaged to Molly Allgood (Maire O'Neill).

1907   Production of *The Playboy of the Western World*. *Playboy* riots in Dublin. Publication of *The Aran Islands* and of *Playboy*.

1908   Publication of *The Tinker's Wedding*. Synge's mother dies.

1909   Synge dies in Dublin on 24 March. First production of *The Tinker's Wedding* at His Majesty's Theatre in London. *Poems and Translations*.

1910   Production of *Deirdre of the Sorrows* at the Abbey Theatre. Publication of *Deirdre*. First edition of the collected works; included in volume 4 are *In Wicklow*, *In West Kerry*, *In the Congested Districts*, and *Under Ether*.

Chapter One

Inner Lands and Outlying Islands

The Approach to the Islands

John Millington Synge was twenty-seven in 1898, the year in which he "fled to the Aran Islands to escape 'the squalor of the poor and the nullity of the rich,'" there to find "among forgotten people a mirror for his bitterness."[1] The transformation that the journey to the islands made in Synge as a writer has become one of the commonplaces of Romantic criticism; and while the story W. B. Yeats tells of his discovery in Paris in December 1896 of the poverty-stricken Synge may serve the necessities of truth, the flair and gesture of Yeats's telling encourage the fond illusion that John Synge sprang full grown out of the Aran Islands—a writer of prose, poetry, and plays, struck to fire by contact with those rocky islands in the west of Ireland.

As Yeats remembered it, his advice to his receptive countryman had been direct and prescriptive: "Give up Paris. You will never create anything by reading Racine, and Arthur Symons will always be a better critic of French literature. Go to the Aran Islands. Live there as if you were one of the people themselves; express a life that has never found expression."[2] According to Yeats's account, the Synge that he found in Paris was, before contact with the Aran Islands, a failure as a writer and as a critic. He had nothing to show for his efforts "but one or two poems and impressionistic essays, full of that kind of morbidity that has its roots in too much brooding over methods of expression and ways of looking upon life, which come, not out of life, but out of literature, images reflected from mirror to mirror."[3]

The implications of Yeats's portrait are clear, for in contrast, the Synge who emerges under Yeats's pen as the creative artist is the man who "went to Aran and became a part of its life, living upon salt fish and eggs, talking Irish for the most part"—the man made vital and productive by contact with a simple, living people and a native, rooted culture. Yeats, in this early account of Synge and the islands, has served only too well that persistent desire among critics and readers to find in Synge's experience a fulfillment of the dicta of *The Lyrical Ballads*; and all that Yeats later wrote about Synge, particularly in the thoughtful "J. M. Synge and the Ireland of his Time," has failed to correct the popular myth.

The Aran Islands (1907), more than any other of Synge's works, has suffered from this myth about Synge the man, for the book has been persistently misread as a document of discovery of attitudes and themes. At best, it has been read merely as a source book for the materials of the plays and as an exercise book for Synge's dramatic methods and language. The failure of critical perspective involved in such a judgment is precisely that which would result from an attempt to read *Walden* as a notebook, a source of Thoreau's attitudes rather than as an artistic expression of them. Only in the sense that all reaction is by definition discovery can *The Aran Islands* yield the conclusion restated by one of Synge's best critics as late as 1962 that the Aran Islands probably gave to Synge "his attitudes to life and the main theme of all his writing."[4]

By the time Synge made his first visit to the Aran Islands on 10 May 1898, almost a year and a half after his first meeting with Yeats in Paris, he was no longer an impressionable young man. He had, in fact, undergone most of the significant formative experiences of his life, including his first operation for the disease that was to terminate his short career little more than a decade later; and it is most doubtful, therefore, that the journeys to Aran gave Synge either his attitudes toward life or his major themes. What the Islands did provide, in a more realistic appraisal, was a means to expression—a setting and an idiom—for attitudes already formulated. Synge found, as Yeats wrote (in 1939, in the last year of his own life), "among forgotten people a mirror for his bitterness."

Through his contact with the islands, Synge became, in the language of Yeats's *Vision,* a man who moved from a "brooding melancholy" and self-centered concern to the receptive man: one who was able to see all of life with a pity "that is inseparable from wisdom." This change is not, as Yeats explains it in his own philosophical work, a matter of acquiring themes or even attitudes; rather, it comes as the result of a discovery of an aesthetic equivalent outside of the self. Synge "had to undergo an aesthetic transformation, analogous to religious conversion, before he became the audacious, joyous, ironical man we know."[5] It is important to realize that Yeats's remarks are undoubtedly overstatements, for his concern is not with the accuracy of a biographical Synge but with the Synge he has chosen as an example of a philosophically conceived type. Overstated or not, Yeats's picture of Synge in *A Vision* is of interest because it emphasizes the fact that it was in the manner of creative relationship and expression that the Aran Islands were important to Synge, not in the matter of themes or essential attitudes toward life or the meaning of human experience. Synge had acquired before his journey to the islands the habit of isolation—physical, spiritual, and social—that enabled him to record and evaluate the lives of a people physically isolated from the rest of the world, spiritually and socially cut off from the world beyond the separating sea, a separation that Synge was ideally equipped to observe and understand. Synge's own alienation from the world of his childhood was never emotionally complete, for, in spite of basic disagreements, his tie to his mother was a deep and lasting one. But he had, even before entrance to Trinity College, Dublin, achieved an intellectual distance from his family and his class, which was ultimately symbolized and, in part, actualized by his self-conscious choice of a home on the Continent and by his intensified study of another language and culture.

In Ireland, Synge's family belonged to the upper-middle-class Protestant Ascendancy, conservative in religion and politics. The death of Synge's father, a barrister, only a year after the birth of John Millington Synge, the last of five children, had left the affairs of the family in the strong hands of his wife, a woman characterized by an unrelenting religious zeal and by an unyielding sense of class obligation.

The family tradition stressed the fact that the Synges had always been the landowning or professional class, with an impressive number of churchmen among them. In fact, Synge's uncle, the Reverend Alexander Synge, as a Protestant missionary, had preceded his nephew to the Aran Islands—a post at which the minister incurred the hostility of the inhabitants when he became concurrently an aggressive, mechanized businessman in competition with the primitive island fishermen.

The earlier history of the family claimed five bishops of the church, and Synge's mother was herself the daughter of a Protestant rector known for his fervent zeal against the Roman Catholics of his county. Synge, as an imaginative child, suffered so much from his mother's intense religious convictions that he later wrote: "the well-meant but extraordinary cruelty of introducing the idea of Hell into the imagination of a nervous child has probably caused more misery than many customs that the same people send missionaries to eradicate."[6] There was little opportunity to escape his mother's supervision of his spiritual progress, for Synge's constant ill health kept him much at home. Except for four years in Dublin schools, his preuniversity education was completed at home with a tutor. The state of his health also cut him off from many usual activities and contacts, and his interests were primarily solitary ones—fishing, walking, seeking specimens for his natural science collections, studying music, reading, and working at languages.

Although, according to legend, the family's patronymic (pronounced *sing*) was awarded the family for a superior vocal performance,[7] even such an apparently innocent interest as music caused Mrs. Synge a great deal of anguish when it became evident that her youngest son intended to pursue it as a career. It was, finally, not his mother's objections but an awareness that his overwhelming shyness would keep him from becoming a performer that caused Synge to give up his intention to make music his life's work. Before turning from music to criticism, however, Synge's study took him to Germany where he began, during his formative years, the sojourn on the Continent that was ultimately to be a source of balance and perspective when he returned to deal with the materials of his native land.

It was Synge's interest in natural history that introduced him to Darwin, a discovery that had a profound effect on the fourteen-year-old boy; and it irrevocably led him, during his college years, to the decision that Christianity did not offer a tenable view of the universe—a decision that completed the intellectual break between Synge and his family and their friends. Although the pressures to conformity were often subtle ones, Synge was enough aware of his anomalous position to copy out in his diary the year after his graduation from Trinity College a couplet from Dryden's *The Hind and the Panther*:

> Of all the tyrannies on human kind
> The worst is that which persecutes the mind.

Symbolic for Synge of the difficult freedom from the tyrannies of society were the tramps and tinkers he saw daily on Ireland's roads. The tramp, remembered from boyhood, came to be symbolic for Synge of the artist, an identification encouraged by the fact that both tramp and artist were outsiders with no accepted place in the comfortable world of the middle class. "In the middle classes the gifted son of a

family is always the poorest—usually a writer or artist with no sense
for speculation—and in a family of peasants, where the average comfort
is just over penury, the gifted son sinks also, and is soon a tramp on
the roadside."[8] The tramp, a recurrent figure in Synge's plays, is, like
the artist, the repository of the experiences of his people; he travels the
roads and tells the tales that have come to him from actual occurrences,
from ancient mythology, and from folktales. He is, like the artist,
invested by the people with a reputation for an understanding of eso-
teric matters "and great knowledge of the fairies." The tramp represents also for Synge a lonely figure, which the man outside society
inevitably must be; and healthful, outdoor life, the gatherings of
friends and audiences tell only part of the story of the life of the tramp.
"In all tramp life plaintive and tragic elements are common even on
the surface."[9] Undoubtedly Synge considered Wordsworth his favorite
poet not only because of Wordsworth's persistent emphasis upon nature
but also because of his treatment of the symbolic values of the solitary
figure.

Although Synge acquired much of his material for the plays from
the various storytellers and tramps he met in his wanderings, he also
had a wide and varied knowledge of classical, French, English, and
Irish literature, history, and mythology. The view of Synge, therefore,
as the primitive, untutored, natural artist is one not justified by the
facts. Synge's performance at Trinity College was not outstanding, but
he did receive prizes in Hebrew and Irish; and his diaries for the years
1892 through 1903 show him to have been constantly involved in
reading (in Greek, Latin, Hebrew, French, German, and Irish) of the
widest kind. It is interesting to note that not only did Synge's extensive
reading provide him a sound general foundation for his work as a writer
but that it also gave him an early, specific acquaintance with the possibilities of the Aran Islands through a reading of William Stokes's life
of George Petrie, in which Stokes records the story of an old Aran
woman who prefigures Maurya in *Riders to the Sea.*

Synge's final decision to abandon music as a career took him from
Germany to France, where he began his new pursuit of languages and
criticism with courses at the Sorbonne in medieval and modern French
literature and in comparative phonetics. His reading of French authors
included Anatole Le Braz and Pierre Loti. Synge's interest in Loti and
in the peasants of Brittany was also of a preparatory nature for his Aran
book, for Synge brought his critical judgment to bear upon Loti's successes and failures in dealing with the Breton peasants.

In short, one must conclude that Synge's creation of literature from his visits to the Aran Islands resulted not so much from what he found in the islands as from what he brought to them. The Aran Islands provided for Synge a stage free of the complexities and false props of "civilization," and against this stark background he saw enacted patterns of reality he had previously observed—a conception of life that is completely and explicitly expressed in a (perhaps imaginary) sketch written in his notebooks before the Aran venture. Synge wrote that, on a train journey from Calais to Paris, he had shared his compartment with eight ballet dancers who fell asleep before the journey was over. Observing their sleeping frailty, Synge became bitterly aware of the irony of the gestures human beings make in the face of a hostile universe—the irony of the human need to make an assertion of beauty—a beauty itself heightened by an awareness of its frail and ephemeral nature:

I looked out every few moments into the wonderful purity of the blue dawn of September, then back again to the gallery of sleeping girls. Is life a stage and all the men and women merely players, or an arena where men and women and children are captives of destiny to be torn with beasts and gladiators—who appear only to destroy and be destroyed. . . .

After awhile I grew so bitter in my strange and solitary watch that I sprang up and cried out to them that we were nearing Paris. They aroused themselves with stiff and dreary expectation. In a few [moments] their tradition of boisterous gaiety restored the chattering that had preceded their hour of slumber. They threw aside their shawls and hats and began to do their hair with combs and looking glasses, plying me with questions about Paris life and theatres, throwing in at times a remark of the rankest obscenity.

Morituri te saluto. The pity I felt changed gradually to admiration as I warmed myself with their high spirits and good humor.[10]

The bitterness that results from Synge's solitary contemplation turns to admiration before the vital assertion of life made by the awakened girls, an admiration for the assertion of personality that Synge consistently expresses throughout his work. The gratuitous gestures of affirmation, which the characters of the plays repeatedly enact, are made only after the action of the play has brought them to a knowledge of the wolfish arena of the world—gestures that are at once statements of human defiance and resignation. "Perhaps a man must have a sense of intimate misery . . . before he can set himself to jeer and mock at the world."[11]

And this knowledge Synge brought with him to the islands, finding there a new metaphor, freed of the fin de siècle weariness of French literature and of the terms of the French symbolists. Much of *The Aran Islands* is concerned with delineating the face of universal reality, and the islands themselves provide a stage remarkable for its simplicity— a way of escaping from Axel's Castle to the hard, unyielding rock of the islands and the eternal presence of the implacable sea.

The Aran Islands

The Aran Islands is composed of a brief introduction and four parts, each part recounting one of the journeys Synge made to the islands in successive summers. The disarming impression of the simplicity of the book's structure is heightened by a brief author's foreword, in which Synge lays out the geography of the three islands and proclaims the truthfulness of his pages: "I have given a direct account of my life on the islands, and of what I met with among them, inventing nothing, and changing nothing that is essential." As a disclaimer of creative accomplishment, the introduction is misleading; like the famous and, perhaps, unfortunate preface to *The Playboy of the Western World,* it grows out of an impulse to insist upon the reality of the world found in these outlying Islands—a world not preconceived in romanticized Irish terms, but one complete and meaningful to the observer willing to accept reality as it exists.

However, Synge's statement that he has invented nothing and changed "nothing that is essential" provides a key to the accomplishment of his first book, which may best be explained as his ability to capture the essence of the islands and to organize highly selected impressions and incidents into a meaningful pattern of reality. Much of the confusion expressed by critics attempting to deal with the accomplishment of *The Aran Islands* rises out of a failure to understand the *kind* of book it is. The book has been variously described as a book of essays, a travel book, or as notebooks;[12] and, in the case of more discreet but perhaps equally uncomfortable critics, the question of *kind* has been sidestepped altogether. A recent study by Mary King sees *The Aran Islands* as "in a continuum with Synge's other confessional prose, the *Autobiography,* the *Vita Vecchia* and the *Etude Morbide,*" even though it differs so radically in tone, content, and language in its treatment of outer and inner worlds. This study also makes an analogy of the form of *The Aran Islands* with musical composition, recalling the fact that Synge had worked hard to become a musician and a composer in the years preceding the composition of *The Aran Islands*.[13] Whatever analogies one may seek, the healthy direction of recent criticism is to take Synge at his word when he writes in a letter of 1907, "I look on *The Aran Islands* as my first serious piece of work."[14] Robin Skelton's *The Writings of J. M. Synge* identifies Synge's book on Aran with *Travels in Arabia Deserta* or *The Seven Pillars of Wisdom,* for "it is in reality a poetic and philosophical interpretation of essential aspects of human life."[15]

It seems helpful to recall that Synge brought a camera to the Aran Islands and that the photographs which survive seek to record nothing picturesque in its own right but rather scenes from the daily life of the inhabitants, and it may be equally helpful to view *The Aran Islands* as a work analogous to the documentary, a term whose meaning has come from the motion picture (a medium not known to Synge during his lifetime), including one made about the Aran Islands by Robert Flaherty, who said that Synge taught him *what* to see.[16] Synge himself does not attempt to define a genre for his book; his concern is with reality and the service of truth, a concern endorsed by the form he has chosen for his work.

That reality can be organized, without benefit of "invention," to present a coherent view of *a* world (and, by extension, of *the* world) is Synge's accomplishment in the Aran Islands. Synge's primary role in presenting the life of the islands to the reader is that of the organizing intelligence, the ideal observer, the selecting eye of the camera. His relationship to his material is essentially that of the cameraman—invisible, perceiving, objective, and amoral. It is Synge's relationship to his material that Yeats has in mind when he speak of *The Aran Islands* as a "book where moral indignation is unknown."[17] This is not to suggest, as study of the documentary mode demonstrates, that an artistically coherent and essentially fictive arrangement is not being expressed. It is the relationship of the maker to the material that is by convention and practice quite different from that of autobiography.

Synge's unique relationship to his material is apparent when we compare the beginning of *Walden* with the beginning of *The Aran Islands.* From its opening lines, Thoreau's account reflects the spirit of his intention: "to brag as lustily as chanticleer in the morning, if only to wake my neighbors up." Synge's record begins quietly, "I am in Aranmor, sitting over a turf fire, listening to a murmur of Gaelic." *Walden* begins with the active expression of intention and will, leading to the famous statement: "I wished to live deliberately, to front only the essential facts of life, and see if I could not learn what it had to teach, and not, when I came to die, discover that I had not lived." Synge, who is not interested in writing his spiritual autobiography, states only, "I am in Aranmor"; and it is only as the recording ("listening") presence that Synge generally enters into the book. The intention of *Walden* brings the reader always back to an awareness of Thoreau the man: the analogy-perceiving intellect; the purposeful, interpreting, insistent experiencer. Since the intention of *The Aran Islands* is quite different, Synge enters actively into his narrative only occasionally, and then usually as the ideal spectator, the dramatist entering the scene momentarily in the choral function. The Synge who appears in *The Aran Islands* is really a character nearly anonymous.

It is necessary to understand Synge's procedure in *The Aran Islands,* but it is equally important to understand that the book is not mere reportage as the introduction and as the conclusions of various critics might suggest. The primary interest of the book is not in the accuracy of the portrayal of peasant life; rather, it is in the universal patterns that reveal themselves against the background of the primitive, rocky islands. Because Synge does not insist on the meaning of the material he chooses to present, the reader should not assume the absence of meaningful patterns in the book.

The four parts of *The Aran Islands*—organized around Synge's journeys to the Islands—begin, in each case, with his arrival and end with his departure: a paradigmatic enactment of the rhythm of existence itself, for between the polarities of arrival and departure, birth and death, human beings enact their difficult roles. Arrival is itself problematic at Aran, for the steamer "sails according to the tide," as Synge reminds us in the beginning of part 1. It sails often in the mist and fog, which conceal and soften for the moment the dreary and desolate rock of the islands. The ever-present extremes and human experience on the islands may be softened for the moment, but the concealing mist becomes at the same time a source of danger to the boats of the sea.

Everything about the islands reminds Synge of the difficulty of existence, of the frailty of human gestures:

A little later I was wandering out along the one good roadway of the island, looking over low walls on either side into small flat fields of naked rock. I have seen nothing so desolate. Grey floods of water were sweeping everywhere upon the limestone, making at times a wild torrent of the road, which twined continually over low hills and cavities in the rock or passed between a few small fields of potatoes or grass hidden away in corners that had shelter. . . . Occasionally I passed a lonely chapel or schoolhouse, or a line of stone pillars with crosses above them and inscriptions asking a prayer for the soul of the person they commemorated.

Synge, with his persistent use of the progressive verb, presents his scene with telling details. The desolation of the islands is established; it remains untouched in any essential way by the pitiful but heroic attempts of human beings to take from this rocky world their necessary sustenance—economic, intellectual, or religious.

Synge's initial impressions are of Aranmor, the first of the islands he visited; and they are intensified by his move inward to Inishmaan "where Gaelic is more generally used, and the life perhaps the most primitive that is left in Europe." The move toward the middle island is made by curragh, the rough canvas canoe that delights Synge because it is a "model that has served primitive races since man first went on the sea." Synge's delight in the primitive leads him to an occasional romanticizing about the life of the people, and some of his reactions seem texts from the Book of William Morris:

Every article on these islands has an almost personal character, which gives this simple life, where all art is unknown, something of the artistic beauty of mediaeval life. The curaghs [sic] and spinning-wheels, the tiny wooden barrels that are still much used in the place of earthenware, the homemade cradles, churns, and baskets, are all full of individuality, and being made from materials that are common here, yet to some extent peculiar to the island, they seem to exist as a natural link between the people and the world about them.

In spite of the occasional rendering of a scene for its picturesque qualities, the cumulative effect of the book is not that of the impressionistic traveler. Instead the effect is to present, by virtue of the very simplicity and primitiveness that are a temptation to quaintness and romanticism, a total vision of a world—one that is to become the background (and foreground, in some cases) of the plays, with all that is merely quaint left behind.

This is a world in which all beauty is seen in relief: "No one who has not lived for weeks among these grey clouds and seas can realize the joy with which the eye rests on the red dresses of the women, especially when a number of them are to be found together." Synge's description of girls washing at the edge of the sea suggests the moment of epiphany in Joyce's *Portrait of the Artist*: "Their red bodices and white tapering legs make them as beautiful as tropical sea-birds." But Synge makes the reader aware of the other side of the coin: that such beauty grows out of the necessities of drought (itself an anomalous hardship on this rainswept island in the sea) and that the practice of washing clothing in sea water is a cause of much of the rheumatism in the islands. If it is human fate to achieve a momentary beauty, there is always a cost to be paid in suffering, and it is a part of the wholeness of Synge's vision that he never fails to insist upon a statement of the opposites that make up the sum of human experience.

In all things the opposites that make up the flux of an uncertain existence are accepted without question by the people of the Aran Islands, and in this their lives are whole. Days of dense fog, which gave to Synge a "strange sense of exile and desolation," may be followed by "the intense insular clearness one sees only in Ireland"; and the sea, which is a source of livelihood for its harvest of fish and of kelp, may one day seem to yield itself to human needs, the next to become the unappeasable destroyer.

Symbolic of the Aran Islanders' ability to adapt to the change that is an accepted part of daily existence are their cottages, built "with two doors opposite each other, the more sheltered of which lies open all day to give light to the interior. If the wind is northerly the south door is opened . . . ; as soon, however, as the wind changes to the south the other door is opened." To yield before change, before necessity, is not, however, to abdicate human emotion—the gesture of personality, energy, and joy. Although the islanders may be temporarily subdued by a week of "sweeping fogs" that reduce their voices to "the whisper of men who are telling stories in a haunted house," they gather in the evening to mend nets and drink poteen, gradually restoring the gaiety that will rise in the face of the fog and rain: "One cannot think of these people drinking wine on the summit of this crumbling precipice, but their grey poteen, which brings a shock of joy to the blood, seems predestined to keep sanity in men who live forgotten in these worlds of mist."

And in Synge's description of the burial of an old woman, which he witnessed on his first trip to the islands, all of the aspects of this life come together for a moving and convincing statement. The burial of the old woman, which takes place after Mass, is itself a mingling of undifferentiated pagan and Christian ceremonies. Before the burial can begin, a hole must be forced (to admit the coffin) through the wall that surrounds the graveyard, and the final act of the men as they leave the burial is the mending of the wall, "talking of anything, and joking of anything, as if merely coming from the boat-slip, or the pier."

Before the hole is closed, however, the keening of the women around the grave has reached such a passionate intensity that it embraces the lot of all the islanders:

This grief of the keen is no personal complaint for the death of one woman over eighty years, but seems to contain the whole passionate rage that lurks somewhere in every native of the island. In this cry of pain the inner consciousness of the people seems to lay itself bare for an instant, and to reveal the mood of beings who feel their isolation in the face of a universe that wars on them with winds and seas. They are usually silent, but in the presence of death all outward show of indifference or patience is forgotten and they shriek with pitiable despair before the horror of the fate to which they all are doomed.

An old woman over eighty is doomed to die—as are all human beings—and her coffin must be passed through a hole broken in the cemetery wall. There is no easy gate even for the dead in such a world, but the mended wall, like life itself, shows no sign when the ceremony is done that an old woman has passed this way.

Grief is a luxury in the islands, a brief but intense rebellion against the human lot, a momentary breaking of the pattern of acceptance. Yet the old women who have recited the keen, even as they sit beside "the roofless shell of the church" in the graveyard are "beginning to talk again of the daily trifles that veil from them the terror of the world." There is, for Synge, in the unflinching acceptance of the islanders, a dignity from which civilization has shut off humankind forever.

Synge follows his account of the old woman's burial by a description of the making of a new field by the men of the house where he resides. The insistent rhythm of life takes its place against the scene of death, and Synge's method of creating a pattern of the contrasts implicit in the life of men and women on the islands is intensified as the book progresses. The demands of life on Aran encompass a wholeness, a completeness, lost in civilization.

The way of life on the islands creates a populace that, in a general way, takes on those aspects that Synge identifies with the lives of tramps and tinkers, who, like the islanders, must take life as they find it, full of contrasts and contradictions: "The continual passing in this island between the misery of last night and splendor of to-day seems to create an affinity between the moods of these people and the moods of varying rapture and dismay that are frequent in artists, and in certain forms of alienation." As Yeats observes, in Synge's Aran Islands were "men and women who under the weight of their necessity lived, as the artist lives, in the presence of death and childhood, and the great affections and the orgiastic moment when life outleaps its limits."[18]

The love of gesture is strong among the islanders, and the telling of stories, anecdotal and folk, is a respected occupation. The ancient Irish reverence for the poet, the maker of fictive patterns, lives still in the islands. The tales are often of outrageous happenings or extravagant gestures, a way of insisting upon a persistent human presence in the universe. Some of the tales Synge hears on the islands are primitive transformations of stories shared by the peoples of the world, and Synge, trained as a comparativist, delights in the evidence before him. The Riddle of the Sphinx is asked Synge by an old man on Aranmor, and Synge hears another tale reminiscent in part of the prototype of *The Merchant of Venice.* "It gave me a strange feeling of wonder to hear this illiterate native of a wet rock in the Atlantic telling a story that is so full of European associations." The stories are not told, as some critics suggest, merely out of a desire on the part of the people to escape from the dreariness and latent horror of daily life into a dream world; there is in all of the tales a strong residue of the astonishment of an unsophisticated people that the doings of people have so long survived in such a world. And this element of wonder is not lost when Synge transforms the tales he hears from the island storytellers into his plays. *The Aran Islands* provides sources for *The Shadow of the Glen, The Playboy of the Western World,* and—through immediate observation—material for *Riders to the Sea.*

In his presentation of the stories of the old men on the islands Synge apprentices himself to the dramatic art, for he steps entirely aside and lets the tale-teller speak in his own idiom both as teller and, in the case of Pat Dirane, as participant. The tale told in the language of the teller has the immediacy of the stage—there is no padding and little description; like the ballad, the tale gives only the bare bones of the dramatic action. And when Pat Dirane concludes with the formula, "that is my story," it is like the falling of a curtain on the stage. (The final sentence of the book, as Synge leaves the islands for the last time, is a formula and effect worthy of Pat Dirane: "The next day I left with the steamer.")

For all the life gestures the people of the islands make (and these include their telling of tales and their extravagance of tongue such as ". . . you're a civil man . . . and here's to your good health and may you live till they make you a coffin out of a gooseberry bush, or till you die in childbed"), death pervades the Aran Islands. As Synge watches the men rhythmically working a dragnet in the surf, he feels that he talks with "men . . . under a judgement of death," who "would be drowned in the sea in a few years and battered naked on the rocks." All human beings are under sentence of death, are riders to the sea, but the sentence has a special immediacy on these islands where death is a part of the daily life.

Part 4 of *The Aran Islands,* like part 1, is dominated by the burial of the dead. But this burial is of a young fisherman, cut off in the prime of life—"a young man who had died in his first manhood, instead of an old woman of eighty." The grief is intensely personal now, and it reaches back as well as forward, for the digging of the grave displaces a skull from the clay. An old woman, mother of the dead man, "took it up in her hands, and carried it away by herself. Then she sat down and put it in her lap—it was the skull of her own mother—and began keening and shrieking over it." The displacement of the long dead for the recent dead and this keening woman are accepted as inevitable by the islanders. It is part of the pattern of unsentimentalized acceptance of necessity, of life and death, like that pattern Synge sees symbolized by the sister of the dead man. She seems to Synge as she sits—keening for the dead while suckling her infant child at her breast—"like a type of the women's life on the islands," a pattern Synge was to use, with similar details, in Maurya's remembrance in *Riders to the Sea.*

The memory of death, as well as expectancy of it, is in the very growth of the islands. "On these rocks, where there is no growth of vegetable or animal life, all the seasons are the same, and this June day is so full of autumn that I listen unconsciously for the rustle of dead leaves."

Humankind, caught between "the two circles of sea and sky" on these barren rocks, might indeed seem, in answer to Synge's earlier questioning, "captives of destiny to be torn with beasts and gladiators—who appear only to destroy and be destroyed." Yet Synge's response is also one of admiration for those who persist in the face of an alien universe, who yield before the larger necessity so that they can, momentarily at least, assert their presence. The Aran Islands bring to Synge an awareness "with immense distress [of] the short moment we have left us to experience all the wonder and beauty of the world."

Observations

In Wicklow, West Kerry and Connemara is not, like *The Aran Islands*, a unified and carefully completed whole. *The Aran Islands* received careful attention from Synge and was, he felt, a finished work in 1902, although a publisher was not found until Elkin Mathews brought out the book in 1907 after the publication of most of the plays. Unlike *The Aran Islands, In Wicklow, West Kerry and Connemara* is a collection of essays and articles—many of them originally published in (and, in part, commissioned by) the *Shanachie* and the *Manchester Guardian* and printed as separate works in the first edition of the collected works the year after Synge's death. As the publisher's note to the collection explains, only a portion of the volume (*In West Kerry*) had been rewritten by Synge before his death. His intention to revise *In the Congested Districts* (*Connemara*) before reprinting was not successfully fulfilled, for his concern for his dramatic work and finally his illness prevented him from completing his revision.

There is much that is of interest in this volume, even in its state of partial completion, for many of Synge's characteristic themes and methods of presentation and the same serviceable prose that worked so admirably in *The Aran Islands* are evident throughout. Nonetheless, this later volume does not have the power of the earlier; it lacks the wholeness, the unity of perception, of *The Aran Islands*.

The series of articles comprising *In the Congested Districts*—originally printed in the *Manchester Guardian* and reprinted as *In Connemara*—records Synge's impressions of life in depressed areas during a trip through the west of Ireland. He remains the dispassionate observer, but he is in these essays an actively evaluating intelligence—judging the successes and failures of the government relief agencies. In general, Synge shows his concern for unrealistic reform imposed on the people from above: "It is far better, wherever possible, to improve the ordinary prosperity of the people till they begin to improve their houses themselves on their own lines, than to do too much in the way of building houses that have no interest for the people and disfigure the country."

The tendency of such aid to disregard the traditions and the lives of the people seemed to Synge to destroy much worth preserving. Synge is not, however, in this series a blindly nostalgic lover of the past at the cost of the present. Instead, he is much concerned to correct the "traditional misconception of the country people" and, having done so, to offer concrete suggestions for the alleviation of their lot. His final essay, "Possible Remedies," offers cool, carefully judged, and very specific suggestions; and it should answer amply those critics who persistently describe Synge as a man without social or political awareness.

In Wicklow and *In West Kerry* (the reworked sections to the book) are of more interest to the student of Synge's art, for the timeless patterns of life and land emerge with something of the same force and meaning that underwrite *The Aran Islands.* An exception to this general concern with those who live on and close to the immediate demands of the land and sea is the selection "A Landlord's Garden in County Wicklow," one of the few occasions in which Synge deals with his own class. Yet his objectivity is such that he is able to express the plight of the land-owning class, a tragedy not so widely recognized as that of the peasant and fisherman. There is not much popular pity for the Irish landlords, "yet one cannot quite forget that they are the descendants of what was at one time, in the eighteenth century, a high-spirited and highly cultivated aristocracy. The broken greenhouses and mouse-eaten libraries, that were designed and collected by men who voted with Grattan, are perhaps as mournful in the end as the four mud walls that are so often left in Wicklow as the only remnants of a farmhouse." In this dead past, or lost tradition, is to be found, Synge suggests, the source of many plays not yet written about Ireland of men who "do not equal their forefathers, . . . [who] used to collect fine editions of *Don Quixote,* Molière, in Spanish and French, and luxuriantly bound copies of Juvenal and Persius and Cicero." This was a topic Synge had tried his hand at in his first play, and to which Yeats was to return again and again in his middle and late verse. Yeats's play *Purgatory* might well have been suggested by Synge's passage were there not immediate and moving sources of this kind of loss in Yeats's own experience.

The sense of loneliness and desolation, which is so much a part of Synge's human landscape, is everywhere evident in this book; and, as in *The Aran Islands,* it heightens awareness of the "ceaseless fading of beauty," an awareness that is perpetual in Synge's work, finding its way even into the statements made by the comedies. Synge knows that the Aran Islands themselves are doomed as a part of the human scene, and he recorded in his notebook at the end of his first visit: "The thought that this island will gradually yield to the ruthlessness of 'progress' is as the certainty that decaying age is moving always nearer to the cheeks it is your ecstasy to kiss."[19]

What is, however, lacking in the lives of most of the poor of the areas of Wicklow, West Kerry, and Connemara is the free play of opposites that Synge saw as yet persisting to create a meaningful pattern of existence in the Aran Islands. Civilization (the "nullity of the rich")—with its attempts to fix life in terms of an artificially imposed morality, to interrupt the natural processes, to stop the normal flux of life—has resulted in the "squalor of the poor" among the peasants of Ireland. The fatal separation from life that the Aran Islanders had not yet experienced at the time of Synge's visit has produced a poverty of mind and heart that can be healed only by the imagination of the artist, which can create, for the moment at least, that sense of the wholeness of existence that Synge found enacted in the Aran Islands.

Chapter Two
First Light: *When the Moon Has Set*

"I wrote one play—which I have never published—in Paris, dealing with Ireland of course, but not a peasant play, before I wrote *Riders to the Sea,*" Synge notes in correspondence to a friend in 1907. Although Synge's extant working papers show him making several starts at early dramas, only *When the Moon Has Set* was brought to completion in a number of versions. He had worked on the play between 1900 and 1903, and had read a two act version to Yeats and Lady Gregory in 1901, which they quite rightly rejected for performance, not only for its failure as drama but, Robin Skelton suggests, because it would have guaranteed a riot in Dublin.[1] They were painfully aware that if *The Countess Cathleen* had produced a riot over the selling of a soul to succor the poor, Synge's play with its rejection of the church, the blasphemy of substituting natural instincts for conventional views of the deity, the successful seduction of a nun, and the personal motivation behind all of the above might well have torn the house down. In the extreme positions of *When the Moon Has Set* Synge had gone far beyond Yeats's in *The Countess Cathleen* with its romantic portrayal of a selfless devotion to Ireland and her poor, which provided its ennobling, if unsettling, motivation. It is easy to understand how great must have been the discomfort that Yeats and Lady Gregory felt upon reading Synge's first completed play.

By 1903 Synge had given the title, *When the Moon Has Set,* to a one-act version of this early play. Yeats, describing in 1909 after Synge's death the play he remembered from the reading of the earlier, longer version, characterizes it as "morbid and conventional though with an air of originality. The only thing interesting about it is that it shows his preoccupation with the thought of death. He knew my opinion about it at the time. It was after its rejection by us he took to peasant work."[2] Yeats's subtle suggestion that he and Lady Gregory had a hand in the cause and effect that turned Synge to the materials of the later plays is typical of Yeats's tendency to try to historicize his part in the

Irish renaissance, but if his comment about Synge's progress is true, it is probably only tangentially so, for Synge was already, by 1901, working on the materials originating from his visits to the Aran Islands and establishing the materials for his first two "peasant" plays. Yeats's description of a preoccupation with death in *When the Moon Has Set* has, in all probability, been partially transformed by his own later notions about Synge's experience, but it was much more evident in the earlier versions than is discernible from the evidence of the one-act version given us by Ann Saddlemyer, which is based on later revisions completed by Synge himself.[3] An emphasis on a reading of the play suggested by Yeats's remarks provides a misleading, if not inaccurate, direction for understanding the late versions, which are clearly life-affirming and preoccupied with waste of human potential rather than with death.

Although *When the Moon Has Set* bears many of the marks of an apprentice piece that was never reclaimable in spite of Synge's continued interest in it, it contains much that is of significance for the student of Synge's artistic development. The play is clearly a precursor, a trial flight, for many of the basic ideas and conflicts that are pervasive throughout the canon as well as a source for a number of phrases and speeches that proved useful to Synge for the later plays. The basic conflict of the play is a struggle familiar to the readers of the canon—the struggle for freedom from the tyranny of religion, the conflict between nature and culture, between natural truths and artificial dogmas. Like many of Synge's plays yet to come, it examines culturally created hierarchies and affirms the awakening of instinctual values and the priceless gift of individual freedom.

The play is in an unlikely place for a Synge play—an Ascendancy country house, representing an aspect of the Anglo-Irish Protestant land owning class that is dying out. In a notebook Synge has the main character, the heir, speak of his uncle, the dead master of the house, in a way that makes clear Synge's conception of the Ascendancy: "What a life he has had. I suppose it is a good thing that this aristocracy is dying out. They were neither human nor divine."[4] This is the theme he takes up again in "A Landlord's Garden in County Wicklow," in which he recognizes the tragedy of the landlord class and the poignancy that attends all moments of change in the social fabric, whether in the upper-class house of a Wicklow landlord or in the Aran Islands as the simple life of the people experiences the beginning of change before forces of modernization and economic exploitation.

The two main characters of Synge's play are Colm, heir to the country house and the old man who has just died, and his distant cousin, Sister Eileen, a nun who has come to nurse her uncle in his last illness; the conflict is over the love between the two young people, which is, of course, forbidden by the vows the nun has taken to her nursing order. The basic situation is one Synge had experienced in his own life, and much of the play seems a therapeutic playing out for Synge of his loss of the love of Cherrie Mathieson, whose strict and strong Protestant religious commitment had caused her to reject Synge as a freethinker. Because the source of the play is so immediate to his own experience, Synge overstates the case without relief; he so loads his side of the argument that for the only time in his dramatic works the result seems an often lifeless preaching rather than an unfolding dramatic tension, and in spite of his best efforts, Sister Eileen is the most wooden character he created. He essentially stages a trial in which the forces of life defeat the forces of repression, which are responsible in the play for madness, lack, and death. He achieves in art a conclusion denied him by real life. According to Synge's nephew and young contemporary, Edward Stephens, Lady Gregory, after reading *When the Moon Has Set,* told Synge that the play failed because he "had written a dramatization of his own life under a thin disguise of fiction, but so direct that it was devoted more to stating, illustrating, and discussing the problems of his particular experience than to interpreting universal emotions."[5]

Yeats is right that death is a force in this play, for the uncle's body lies in an adjoining room and is felt in its absence as a force, a memento mori at least, in the same way that the Catholic church is felt as an incontrovertible and absolute force when a telegram arrives from the mother superior summoning Sister Eileen back to the convent. (It must have given Synge pleasure to have Eileen leave her discarded nun's veil in the room where the dead man's body lies at the end of the play.) Both death and the repressive tyranny of the church work in dramatic terms, however, to emphasize the need to accept the gifts of life while it is still possible to do so. Speaking for this point of view, the young heir to the estate aligns himself with the sanity of nature and the fecundity of life, and in his triumphant final speech, he sounds like a nascent D. H. Lawrence: "I, the male power, have overcome . . . the reader of the saints. From our harmonized discord new notes will rise. . . . we will assimilate with each other. . . . We have incarnated God, and been a part of the world. That is enough."

Colm has had more than his share of help in bringing Sister Eileen to the point of renouncing her vows and accepting him, for part of the business of the play involves the revelation that a local madwoman is Mary Costello, once a proud beauty from a formerly great family. This identification is followed by the revelation that although the deceased master of the house had been willing to go against convention in order to marry a woman whose family has now sunk below his station in life, Mary "broke it off because he did not believe in God." She subsequently goes mad from her instinctive knowledge that the church has been responsible for an unfulfilled life, which she translates into guilt and grief for the children she did not have, although in her madness she fills that lack with their presence: "There are five children, five children that wanted to live, God help them, if the nuns and the priests with them had let me be. . . . They're always nice your honour, with clean faces, and nice frocks on them."

Although Mary Costello has created a kind of plenitude through her madness, her rejected suitor, the deceased uncle, had completely withdrawn from the world and spent a lifetime grieving for lost possibility. Synge plays insistently with the traces of what might have been. The picture of Mary Costello as a young and beautiful girl hangs over the fireplace and the contrast between what might have been and what has been distorted by the death-dealing dictates of the church is clear when, preceded by the sound of her hysterical laughter, the demented woman enters the room. Seemingly oblivious, she goes to a bureau in the corner, takes out two rings that she puts on her hand, and begins the motion of throwing a bridal dress over her head. After becoming aware of the others, she finally gives the rings to Sister Eileen in exchange for the nun's cross and admonishes Eileen once again: "Let you mind the words I was saying and give no heed to the priests or the bishops or the angels of God, for it's little the like of them . . . knows about women or the seven sorrows of the earth."

When Sister Eileen yields to the forces of nature, Colm's persuasion, and the terrifying exemplum that has been played out before her, it is Mary Costello's abandoned wedding dress she dons, and the rings at last find their proper, if long-thwarted, use when Colm performs, appropriately as the moon sets and the sun rises, a secular ceremony, "In the name of the Summer, and the Sun, and Whole World, I wed you as my wife." The simplicity of Colm's ceremony and the appeal to the sanction of all that is natural becomes an ironic inversion and a final rejection of the meaningless rituals of the hegemonic power of the church.

It is interesting to watch Synge struggling in this first play to find symbols for the oppositions he attempts to make dramatically compelling. One example is the "wedding" dress that is green in color—at one with nature, or perhaps, with Ireland, which will survive the destruction of the society based on the hierarchy enforced by the inhabitants of the Big Houses. The taking of the dress and the rings from the press and their proper use seems almost too easy a symbolic statement of the release of that which has been buried, as if the passionate potential of those for whom they originally had been a promise of life-giving relationship is finally retrieved for the next generation in the presence of the dead body of the old man. The moon itself, traditionally linked with chastity and coldness, must set so that the sun, symbol of growth and fecundity, may rise. The triumph of the male principle over the female is also celebrated, however consciously, in the symbolic nexus that begins with the title Synge ultimately settled on for his play and ends with the insistence of the final speech.

In *When the Moon Has Set* Synge tries to bring a somewhat intransigent subject matter into dramatic terms and to find ways to master his stagecraft, but one problem inherent to the play that he cannot resolve is the crucial problem of its language. It is through Colm, the young Ascendancy heir, that Synge must communicate to the audience his deep commitment to the life-giving forces of nature and hatred of the repressive forces of convention, here represented by the church, which lead to barrenness and grief. Colm's choosing a commitment to the natural world is ideologically perhaps more forceful because he speaks from a privileged social position, yet his status becomes the crux of the language problem for the reader or hearer of the play. The standard, educated English of his speeches inevitably sounds stiff and preachy when set against the language of the "people"—Mary Costello and the servant, Bride. When Colm says, "Without love this world would be a loathsome sandhill, and a soul without love is not a great deal better. . . . I want to hear you, your voice will have a new cadence from today," the stiffness and stuffiness of the language seems at variance with its intent, and mocks Synge's own mastery of language in the play.

One has only to set Colm's argument to his beloved, "Why will you worship the mania of the saints when your own existence is holier than they are. People renounce when they have not the power to retain; you have power and courage. . . . I implore you to use them" against Mary Costello's plea to Sister Eileen, "There's great marrying in the world but it's late we were surely, and let yourselves not be the same" to hear where the power and life of the language falls. Colm's language works against Synge's dramatic intentions. In this early play Synge's problem is similar to that of D. H. Lawrence when he gives Birken, for example, in *Women in Love* (a work with similarities to Synge's play) philosophical messages to deliver. The problem that Synge fails to solve here he never faces again. The plays to follow attain a unity that begins with and centers in language.

Chapter Three

"The Tyrannies on Human Kind": *The Shadow of the Glen*

Sources and Resources

Synge's first staged play was *The Shadow of the Glen,* which followed Yeats's *The King's Threshold* on the night of 8 October 1903 at Molesworth Hall, Dublin, where the Irish National Theatre company had found a temporary home. Written during a summer in Wicklow in 1902, at about the same time as *Riders to the Sea* and the early drafts of *The Tinker's Wedding,* this first performance of a Synge play incurred the kind of hostile reaction that was to pursue Synge's dramatic career until his death. Maud Gonne, whose championship of Irish causes had seemed from the first as fanatical to Synge as it was later to appear to Yeats, walked out during the performance in protest against Synge's portrayal of Irish womanhood, and the *Daily Independent and Nation* agreed that the play was a "farcical libel on the character of the average decently reared Irish peasant woman."[1]

The persistent reaction to Synge's plays on the part of those whose vision was limited by any of the tyrannies that "persecute the mind" was not of the same kind as the theological "hyperniceness" involved in the controversy over Yeats's *The Countess Cathleen*; but the same charge of "foreign" influence was also brought against Yeats's play. Even when religious defensiveness did enter into the criticism of Synge's plays, it followed hard upon a sense of outrage more basic to the general human situation—an outrage that proclaimed aloud Synge's ability to project upon the stage a conflict usually hidden beneath the stereotypes of middle-class Irish life. It is interesting to note in this context that Ibsen's *A Doll's House,* in which the heroine (also a Nora) rebels against a stereotyped role as wife and mother, challenged middle-class preconceptions about marriage in exactly the same way as Synge's play and that it also met on every hand the same kind of angry responses from audience and critics.[2]

A part of Synge's unwillingness to accept stereotypes for reality, on stage or off, included his refusal to accept the traditional dramatic portrayal of the Irish peasantry as a happy, easygoing, drink-contented breed. The desire to accept only that view of life verifiable by his experience led Synge to reject the stage Irishman as a subject for comedy—a rejection that was the general policy of the Abbey playwrights. The Irishman that Synge drew in his first comedy was, instead, the small landowner, the man of the land corrupted by the middle-class values he had made his own, living out a life in which economic poverty had been traded for poverty of spirit—a deprivation much worse than physical hunger. In this early short play Synge managed to say enough to call forth an angry reaction from those who wanted the false picture of the historical stage Irishman answered not with the truth but instead with some sort of "ideal" Irishman who would be equally false.

Synge's ability to compress a great deal into a very short space is an achievement he has mastered in his first staged play. *The Shadow of the Glen* is, like *Riders to the Sea,* a one-act play, a form that seemed to come naturally to Synge. His early and apparently effortless mastery of the one-act play should not be cause for surprise, however; for the one-act play is, like the short story, a form that depends upon the presentation of a single incident, a single mood—the creation of a moment that invokes a much wider world. The unit with which Synge first worked for the stage is easily recognized as being essentially the same unit with which he built *The Aran Islands,* a book made up of a series of linked, poignant moments, memorable pictures or stories. Each is presented independently without comment or preface and grows, finally, into a total structure.

Significantly, *The Shadow of the Glen* is itself a dramatic rendering of a tale recorded by Synge in *The Aran Islands* and one he had heard from Pat Dirane, an old man who died before Synge's second visit to the islands. The story of an unfaithful wife, it echoes a motif recurrent not only in Irish folktales but also in world literature. The source for the play was identified by Arthur Griffith in the *United Irishman* as a "corrupt version of that old world libel on womankind—the Widow of Ephesus." Griffith's charge against Synge's play laid down the general lines of attack to be used against Synge in his lifetime: that his work was un-Irish, that it was of "foreign" origin and therefore suspect, and that Synge himself had been corrupted by his study of foreign literatures, particularly by the "decadent" French.

Synge's letter in reply to Griffith's editorial was the first of a number of such assertions about his firsthand knowledge of his Irish source and about his general treatment of the Irish peasant character. As Synge pointed out, his play differed "essentially from any version of the story of the Widow of Ephesus" with which he was acquainted; and, as a part of his defense, Synge enclosed an account of the story as he had heard it from his Aran source. The story, which is also that given in *The Aran Islands,* is much closer to the story of the Widow of Ephesus than is Synge's play; for in the play the character of Nora Burke makes it clear that it is not sexual conquest she seeks, nor mere security any longer, but, instead, human companionship and imaginative fulfillment. Synge's Nora is not a woman "wearing her lusts upon her sleeve, a being all appetite and no faculty" as Daniel Corkery exclaimed in his 1931 study of Synge.[3] In an obvious and significant reversal of his source, Nora offers the tramp the use of the bed so that she may have an opportunity to talk to the young herdsman in the privacy of the parlor.

Synge's reaction to the charges of unhealthy sexuality in his play is contained in the draft of a letter to be sent to Stephen MacKenna: "Heaven forbid that we should have morbid, sex-obsessed drama in Ireland, not because we have any peculiar sanctity, which I utterly deny   blessed unripeness is sometimes akin to damned rottenness, see percentage of lunatics in Ireland and causes thereof—but because it is bad as drama and is played out. On the French stage you get sex without its balancing elements. On the Irish stage you get the other elements without sex. I restored sex and the people were so surprised they saw the sex only."[4]

In Pat Dirane's story which Synge records in *The Aran Islands,* Dirane tells of being caught, like the tramp of the play, on the road in a hard rain and of seeking shelter in a lighted house:

Then she took me in and told me her husband was after dying on her, and she was watching him that night.

"But it's thirsty you'll be, stranger," says she. "Come into the parlour."

Then she took me into the parlour—and it was a fine clean house—and she put a cup, with a saucer under it, on the table before me with fine sugar and bread.

When I'd had a cup of tea I went back into the kitchen where the dead man was lying, and she gave me a fine new pipe off the table with a drop of spirits.

"Stranger," says she, "would you be afeared to be alone with himself?"

"Not a bit in the world, ma'am," says I; "he that's dead can do no hurt."

Then she said she wanted to go over and tell the neighbours the way her husband was after dying on her, and she went out and locked the door behind her.

I smoked one pipe, and I leaned out and took another off the table. I was smoking it with my hand on the back of my chair—the way you are yourself this minute, God bless you—and I looking on the dead man, when he opened his eyes as wide as myself and looked at me.

"Don't be afraid stranger," said the dead man; "I'm not dead at all in the world. Come here and help me up and I'll tell you all about it." . . .

"I've got a bad wife, stranger, and I let on to be dead the way I'd catch her goings on."

Then he got two fine sticks he had to keep down his wife, and he put them at each side of his body, and he laid himself out again as if he was dead.

In half an hour his wife came back and a young man along with her. Well, she gave him his tea, and she told him he was tired, and he would do right to go and lie down in the bedroom.

The young man went in and the woman sat down to watch by the dead man. A while after she got up and "Stranger," says she, "I'm going in to get the candle out of the room; I'm thinking the young man will be asleep by this time." She went into the bedroom, but the divil a bit of her came back.

Then the dead man got up, and he took one stick, and he gave the other to myself. We went in and saw them lying together with her head on his arm.

The dead man hit him a blow with the stick so that the blood out of him leapt up and hit the gallery.

That is my story.

This tale has enough convincing parallels recorded by the Irish Folklore Commission to confirm the fact that it was a tale genuinely current in the West of Ireland,[5] and Corkery notes the presence of a short story with the same theme in *Once a Week* in 1860.[6] Lady Gregory even discovered during the American tour of the Abbey Players several Irish immigrants who could remember the same story as a hearthtale from their childhood in Ireland.

What is more important, however, than a discussion of the play's origin in the vindication of Synge (a discussion that unintentionally but inevitably dignifies Griffith's old charge of the derivative nature of the play) is Synge's transformation of Pat Dirane's tale into a compelling one-act drama. Many of the details of the Aran story are present in Synge's play. Other details are first recorded in *The Aran Islands,* such as the tramp's request for a needle and his comment that "there's great safety in a needle, lady of the house." This notion derives from a folk superstition told Synge by Pat Dirane that a needle provides protection against fairies and spirits: "'Take a sharp needle,' he said, 'and stick it in under the collar of your coat, and not one of them will be able to have power on you.'" Nevertheless, the characters of Nora Burke and the tramp are not provided in the source in the way that they emerge under Synge's direction; and it is within these characters that the meaning of the play is realized. There is also in the play as Synge created it much of the thematic material that he was to develop and explore further in *The Playboy of the Western World*.

The Quick and the Dead

In *The Shadow of the Glen* the motives for Dan Burke's action grow out of the same kind of fertile but limited imagination that the Mayo men of the later play possess. Assuming that infidelity is the inevitable result of the marriage of January and May, the old man feigns death so that he can observe and trap his young wife. Synge provides the audience, however, with knowledge about Nora that is denied to the limited mind of the old man, although he overhears exactly what the audience learns.

In a country where late marriages are a part of an economic and traditional necessity, Nora Burke, who has been trapped by the standards of her world into a loveless marriage with an old man, has learned how inadequate to human needs are merely "a bit of a farm, and cows on it, and sheep on the back hills"[7] to fence against old age. And, as a result of her knowledge, she has become a creature of unfulfilled potentiality, a person who, by her dissatisfaction, questions the standards of a society that would say that a sound house, a marriage, and a source of income are enough for humankind. Her questioning involves a conflict to become familiar to the audiences of *The Playboy of the Western World*, and the young herdsman, Michael Dara, on whom Nora momentarily pins her hopes, is an embryonic Shawn Keogh, cowardly and full of the suspicions and the materialistic meanness of the corrupted peasant mind. He even appeals to Nora to save him from Dan Burke's wrath just as Shawn Keogh seeks a similar refuge from Christy Mahon's wrath in *The Playboy of the Western World*. The man that Michael Dara is now and will become with age is clearly mirrored by the old man in the last moments of the play, as they sit sharing whiskey and opinions.

Dan Burke has a right to be suspicious about his wife's discontentment, but he translates her longings for human companionship and a wider world for imaginative growth into a conventional and easy explanation of her restlessness, which is, for the limited imagination, simple infidelity. On the other hand, Patch Darcy, whose name resounds almost thematically throughout the play, represents that wider world Nora longs for, and the true meaning of Darcy's life and death suggests something valorized by both Nora and the Tramp but viewed with suspicion by Dan Burke and Michael Dara. The reaction of the characters to Darcy becomes a means of suggesting the nature of the conflict in the play. Patch Darcy has special values that emerge in the play; and, although he met his death in madness, he at least ventured out from the small world of the safe farm in the glen. He was a "great man," we are told by the tramp; and Nora, who understands, agrees. Their unsupported insistence on Patch Darcy's greatness is the result of Synge's attempt to suggest a wider range of meaning than he is able to formulate in dramatic terms in this early play. Patch Darcy was a good shepherd, an able man with the mountain ewe, the animal that causes Michael Dara such symbolic and actual difficulties. Darcy had control over the natural elements and an instinctive knowledge of them. His knowledge and imaginative sympathy included an understanding of human needs, for he stopped to speak to Nora on his way "passing up or passing down," alleviating her loneliness until his death. Whereas Michael Dara sees only money in his herds, Patch Darcy "would walk through five hundred sheep and miss one of them," for Darcy is like Milton's Lycidas, the true shepherd, whose prototype is Christ. His relationship to his sheep is not measured by their price at market; he was a great man, the tramp says, because there was "never a lamb from his own ewes he wouldn't know before it was marked." Darcy's relationship to Nora was marked by his knowledge of her need, and he dies trying to save his sheep from a fearful storm that drives him, in his human despair, into madness. We are told without further comment that his body is not found for three days; his resurrection is in the legend he has become, in the language of Nora and the tramp.

The implication established by Synge, is that Darcy was not of the careful, small, materialistic breed represented by Dan Burke and the young herdsman, who can drive a hard bargain but not the mountain ewe. Like Yeats's Red Hanrahan, even in his madness Darcy has left legend behind him; and Synge intends to suggest that his madness came from excess, largeness, courage, daring—a madness to be opposed to the meanness and smallness of the "sane" world that believes "a bit of a farm" and a good price for lambs make up the sum of existence. Patch Darcy is a hint of that ideal of the poet in *The Playboy of the Western World*—"fine, fiery fellows with great rages when their temper's roused"—the free, extraordinary personality that is associated with the poet and the man of extravagant gesture as well as with the man of physical prowess (compare Christy Mahon's success at the games with Darcy's ability to run from "this to the city of Dublin and never catch for his breath"). What Synge only suggests in this early play is to become a part of the dramatic structure by the time of the writing of *The Playboy of the Western World*.

The function of the tramp in *The Shadow of the Glen* becomes a crucial one, one dependent upon an understanding of the conflict of the worlds of the play—the world of Dan Burke and that of Patch Darcy—a conflict that Synge has not dramatically realized in this play. The tramp, like the setting of the play, is described by Synge in the essays of *In Wicklow*. He is the solitary, the man who has rejected the confines of civilization for that life which is free and healthful. "In all the circumstances of this tramp life there is a certain wildness that gives it romance and a peculiar value for those who look at life in Ireland with an eye that is aware of the arts also." The tramp represents, in Irish life, an example of the kind of variation from the ordinary that is meaningful for the arts. This art is, "however, founded on the variations which are a condition and effect of all vigorous life"; it is not to be confused with that "founded on the freak of nature, in itself a mere sign of atavism or disease," and, therefore, never universal. "To be quite plain, the tramp in real life, Hamlet and Faust in the arts, are variations; but the maniac in real life and Des Esseintes and all his ugly crew in the arts, are freaks only."[8]

The tramp, then, represents that joy and reality of which Synge speaks in the preface of *The Playboy of the Western World* and which he finds necessary to the healthy stage. The tramp has in this early play, however, a value that is never clearly defined by the play; and the ending of the drama, in which the tramp takes Nora off with him onto the roads, seems somewhat romanticized and not wholly justified by the action of the play. The wiser Synge of *The Playboy of the Western World* understood that Pegeen Mike (who is always the publican's daughter for all her longing to escape the smallness of her life) would not rise to the challenge represented by the playboy, and the more experienced playwright was also able to make the playboy grow before the eyes of his audience—to dramatize rather than to talk about the conflicts of the play and the values that are involved.

Although Synge leaves us with a question about Nora's freedom to make a choice, the world into which the tramp takes Nora is a world in which life may at least be lived, and it will be a "vigorous life" rather than the small and wasted life that she has known with Dan Burke: "making yourself old with looking on each day, and it passing you by." Like the Aran Islanders, who have learned to yield before the changing of the wind, the tramp will teach Nora to take what experience gives: "You'll be saying one time: 'It's a grand evening, by the grace of God,' and another time: 'It's a wild night, God help us; but it'll pass, surely.'"

Nora's dissatisfaction with her life in the shadow of the glen has been heightened by her awareness of the shortness of human existence and the ravages of mortality; for she, a passive spectator at life's door, has watched her childhood friends move through decay toward death, completely worn out with the life imposed upon them: "Isn't it a long while I am sitting here in the winter and the summer, and the fine spring, with the young growing behind me and the old passing." There has been no life in the farmhouse with Dan Burke, who is as cold in this world as he will be in death; but the tramp can offer Nora an alternative: "it's fine songs you'll be hearing when the sun goes up," instead of the "old fellow wheezing, the like of a sick sheep, close to your ear." And from the grouse, the owls, the larks, and the "big thrushes" Nora will hear no tales "of getting old like Peggy Cananagh, and losing the hair off you, and light of your eyes." the *lived* life is, for Synge, the natural life—the expressive, the vigorous life in which an individual's best possibility is in his or her acceptance of the whole with its risks, instead of the safely hedged part of existence that society seeks to substitute for the whole range of potential experiences. The person who is fully alive is always conscious of, but has no time to regret, death, which is, finally, a part of the natural cycle.

Nowhere in the play is the conflict between the opposing attitudes toward existence better dramatized than in the scene in which Michael Dara sits counting the "dead" man's money on the table before him while Nora tries to tell him about her sense of the waste of such a life. Here the contrast between the sensitive and the insensitive is effectively drawn, a conflict that preoccupied Synge in all of his work. The insensitive, the materialistic, the "acceptable" are represented in the play by an appropriately "dead," suspicious old man and by a cowardly, grasping young man; and those who ask more of life must be cast out from such a world. The life of *having* has no tolerance for the life of *being or becoming,* as the end of *The Playboy* also shows. Although Nora has her doubts about the vision of the new life that the tramp draws for her, there is no other choice. She accepts her fate with him, knowing as Synge intends his audience to know, that however difficult this new world may be, it will be better than that she leaves behind. The issues are oversimplified, but they are clear.

Synge's understanding of the difficult situation of women in Ireland, forced by economic necessity to make loveless marriages, is clear in his portrayal of Nora, who essentially is passive, unable to experience personal growth or satisfaction until she is forced by her aged husband to leave the tomb that is the house in the dark shadow of the glen. One of the ironies of the play is that by feigning death, Dan Burke provides a metaphor for the reality of Nora's life and unwittingly opens the door of possibility for Nora. She is free not only of Dan Burke but also of Michael Dara, the pretender to the throne and the hand of the lady of the house, for he is caught both by his own greed (he sees Nora only in commodity terms as the provider of good grazing for his flock) and, ironically, by the machinations of his double, the old man playing dead. In the scene at the end of the play, as the two sit drinking together the visual image in the economy of Synge's dramaturgy suggests that he takes Nora's place in an equally strange ménage. A central metaphor of the play is that of the wake, or a mock wake, in which Patch Darcy rather than Dan Burke is eulogized,[9] and when the old man stages his "resurrection" and drives Nora from the house, we experience the irony that the true resurrection, the only one possible for Synge, belongs to Nora.

From *The Aran Islands* on, we find Synge constantly praising what partakes of the natural rhythms of existence and condemning all that would attempt to fix life in some kind of preconceived pattern or to impose any rigid, restrictive scheme—moral, social, religious—upon the world. The conflict suggested by *The Shadow of the Glen* and by most of Synge's other plays renders unacceptable the usual identification of his plays as "folk drama." Only *Riders to the Sea* might be called with any justice at all a "folk drama," and it is so much more than this that the label becomes as meaningless in context as it is inaccurate in the case of the comedies. That life represented by *The Aran Islands,* the sturdy life of the people, is not present in the comedies except as an opposition to the debased, "civilized" world that holds the center of the stage. Synge, who is concerned with delineating the "tyrannies of mankind," can only suggest that existence which might be opposed to them; for it is, by definition, too large to be portrayed upon the comic stage. The life that fits the stage is the one defined by social pressures; the life that people *ought* to claim as their own always exists somewhere beyond the wings. Only in *The Playboy of the Western World* does Synge come close to resolving his problem of presenting a working dialectic that can be dramatically embodied upon the stage.

Synge's characters in *The Shadow of the Glen* are common people, but the conflict of the play grows out of the unsatisfactory nature of middle-class values that have been taken over whole cloth by the small farmers of Wicklow. Frank O'Connor is partially right, however, in his observation that Synge's conclusion of sending Nora off with the tramp is one "which is arbitrary and comes not out of life but literature—middle-class literature."[10]

The plays of Synge, Yeats, and Lady Gregory were, as O'Connor observes, a "challenge to the mob" because they contain a view of life that "holds that nothing is settled, that everything must be created anew, that there is no such thing as progress, and that all utopianism is a curse. Ideas that run counter to the whole middle-class conception of life."[11] It is interesting to find a comment of Yeats in "The Death of Synge" that supports O'Connor's contention and moves the reaction to Synge's work out of that often-misleading Irish context in which it received its loudest and harshest judgments. Yeats notes that during a performance of *The Playboy of the Western World* at Stratford-on-Avon, a large part of the audience was shocked precisely "because it was a self-improving, self-educating audience, and that means a perverted and commonplace audience."[12]

Perhaps Synge's choice of setting for his plays has been responsible for misleading critics into considering them as folk dramas. Certainly, the setting—the surrounding world—enters strongly into all his plays; and "the influence of a particular locality" serves to accentuate certain aspects of the human condition. In his essay "The Oppression of the Hills," from *In Wicklow,* Synge describes the same world that Nora describes when she asks, "what good is a bit of a farm . . . when you do be sitting looking out from a door the like of that door, and seeing nothing but the mists rolling down the bog, and the mists again, and they rolling up the bog, and hearing nothing but the wind crying out in the bits of broken trees were left from the great storm, and the streams roaring with the rain?" The oppression of the hills was much in Synge's mind when he wrote *The Shadow of the Glen,* for the embryonic account of Patch Darcy's death is also present in this essay: "They found his body on the mountain, and it near eaten by the crows." Nature for Synge is not benevolent; it is a part of the human being's ultimate defeat; but, unlike society, nature permits fullness of expression in defeat. Unlike society with its pressures for conformity, nature is a worthy antagonist that makes it possible for the protagonist to grow into fullness of being. People, for Synge, are oppressed, made small, only when they feign death to preserve a little life, or huddle in their houses and count their coins.

Synge himself in the Aran Islands had to learn the "natural walk of man," for his booted foot was soon bruised on the rocks of the islands, the boots throwing his weight on the heels of his feet. Synge observed that, for the islanders, "the absence of the heavy boot of Europe has preserved to these people the agile walk of the wild animal. . . . Their way of life has never been acted on by anything much more artificial than the nests and burrows of the creatures that live around them, and they seem, in a certain sense, to approach more nearly to the finer types of our aristocracies—who are bred artificially to a natural ideal—than to the labourer or citizen." It is to this natural life of man that Synge sends Nora, however unconvincingly in dramatic terms, at the end of *The Shadow of the Glen.*

Chapter Four
Riders to the Sea

The Whole Fabric

From *The Aran Islands,* which Synge called his "first serious piece of work," he learned "to write the peasant dialect and dialogue" which were to be so effective in his plays. The Aran Islands taught Synge a great deal more than his remarkable use of language, however, for out of his experiences of the islands and the creation of a book about them came the sense of peasant life that pervades all the plays and gives to Synge the language for a coherent expression of his attitudes toward life. Nowhere is this sense of peasant life so evident in Synge's work as in *Riders to the Sea,* a play begun during the same summer as *The Shadow of the Glen* but not staged until 1904, a year after Synge's first-produced play had tried the boards of Molesworth Hall. The setting, the colors, the action, the attitudes, the symbols, the rhythms of the keening women, of fate, and of the sea—all these are present in *The Aran Islands*; and they are the raw materials that Synge compressed, fused, and shaped anew in the creation of the one-act tragedy *Riders to the Sea.* The strong Irish folklore element in *Riders to the Sea* is explored at length by Declan Kiberd in *Synge and the Irish Language,* a study that makes clear the strong roots of the play in Irish folk belief and myth,[1] elements that underpin and work in the play alongside those classical and Christian aspects that are readily available to the ordinary playgoer. The strength of the play is that it can accommodate all the belief systems and the symbols they provide without a sense of Synge's overt manipulation.

The intense perfection of this short play stresses more than any other work the nature and quality of Synge's artistic accomplishment, although the bitter, society-directed irony of the comedies is not present; and, for this reason, *Riders to the Sea* holds in some respects a special place in relation to Synge's work as a whole. The sense of place and of a people is strong in this play, as in all Synge's plays; and, on one level, *Riders to the Sea* may be viewed (as the other plays may not) as "folk drama," for there is none of the insistently foregrounded social comment on the conflict of the needs of the individual and the restrictive demands of society, a conflict that is an overt part of the thematic material in most of the other plays. Predictably enough, *Riders to the Sea* is the only one of Synge's plays presented during his lifetime that did not occasion angry denunciations from audiences in Ireland. In fact, according to Lennox Robinson in *Ireland's Abbey Theatre,* the reception of the play was largely an indifferent one.

Riders to the Sea cuts behind the surface concerns of life to engage its characters in the most elemental kind of struggle—that for existence. The theme is stated with an artistic finality that leaves no room for argument, and the play succeeds because Synge has completely integrated all its aspects. There are no holes in the fabric of the drama; as in the best poetry there are no parts separable from the whole. It is this play of all of Synge's for which Una Ellis-Fermor's judgment of his particular genius seems most appropriate: "Synge is the only great poetic dramatist of the [Irish] movement; the only one, that is, for whom poetry and drama were inseparable, in whose work dramatic intensity invariably finds poetic expression and the poetic mood its only full expression in dramatic form."[2]

The most immediate effect of *Riders to the Sea* is its sense of inevitability and economy. There is nothing that is extraneous; there is nothing that is without meaning in a total pattern, a pattern that works toward an almost symphonic integration of theme and expression. there is no insistence on Synge's part on his meaning; everything in the work grows out of the natural life that he observed in the Aran Islands, and this realistic equivalent for all that happens is a part of the play's inevitability and its art.

The scene is a simple one: "Cottage kitchen, with nets, oilskins, spinning-wheel, some new boards standing by the wall, etc." This is the small world of the play, which will, before Synge has finished his half hour on the stage, bring into the cottage the world beyond that human desire cannot enclose, cannot control. All of the play is pervaded by a sense of a large, natural atmosphere—of the elemental presence of sky and landscape, shore and sea, storm and rocks—although the whole scene is limited to the confines of the cottage kitchen. The immediate canvas is small, but the picture Synge presents has tragic intensity and depth. The sea, which has claimed the lives of all of the men of the family, fills the small kitchen with its presence, just as it fills it with death before the quiet resignation with which the play ends—a quiet that the audience feels in the cessation of struggle like a silence on the sea itself at the storm's end.

In every aspect of his play Synge has perfected the micro-macrocosm relationship. The small world of the cottage kitchen contains the puny attempts of human beings to make a home of the boundless, alien world of the sea. And the island itself, surrounded by the unfriendly sea, becomes a paradigm for life, but one in which the bitter demands of existence speak with a foreshortened insistence: "In the big world the old people do be leaving things after them for their sons and children, but in this place it is the young men do be leaving things behind for them that do be old." All people are riders to the sea, as the audience is reminded by an echo of the conclusion of Sophocles' *Oedipus* in Maurya's final words: "No man at all can be living for ever, and we must be satisfied."

The three women in the play, who are reminiscent of the three Fates of mythology, are an analogy ironic and meaningful in their *inability* to control; but Synge makes his comment effective precisely because he does not insist upon it. It is a parallel that, like many factors in the play, operates without an insistence upon a conscious awareness on the part of the audience. The three women can only endure, await the deprivation and loss that is their lot at the edge of the sea. Nevertheless, the play opens with Cathleen at the spinning wheel, spinning rapidly, as Nora brings in the shirt and stocking found on a drowned man. The clothing is identified as that belonging to their brother Michael, for Nora had dropped four stitches in the knitting of his stocking. The presence of the spinning woman and the attention given to the dropped stitches recalls the classical analogue in a persistent way throughout the play. The pattern of fate is being spun and woven as inexorably in *Riders to the Sea* as in any classical tragedy, and Synge has provided the dramatic symbol, the stage equivalent, which is inevitable, natural, and right. In the same unobtrusive manner we have the cutting of the knot on the bundle of clothing brought from the sea. "Give me a knife, Nora; the string's perished with the salt water, and there's a black knot on it you wouldn't loosen in a week." The shadows of Clotho, Lachesis, and Atropos quietly rise behind the figures of Synge's fate-ridden women.

Synge's symbolism is not only classical in origin, it is also specifically Christian in its evocation. The source of the vision that Maurya sees of the drowned Michael riding behind the son soon to die may be found in *The Aran Islands* in a story about an accident in loading horses on a hooker; in it an old woman saw her drowned son riding on one of the horses, which was caught by a young man who was, then, himself drowned in the sea. Like almost everything in *Riders to the Sea,* the raw material for this incident is present in *The Aran Islands,* but in the prose work Synge presents an unimpassioned telling, which is unified, focused, and given wider context for the purposes of his dramatic re-creation. In Maurya's vision of Bartley on the red mare, followed on the gray pony by Michael, already nine days drowned in the far north, Synge uses the Aran material to invoke wider echoes for his audience—those of the horsemen of the Book of Revelation: "And I looked, and behold a pale horse; and his name that sat on him was Death."

Bartley's death is for Maurya at this moment an accomplished fact, and she withholds from him the loaf that she has taken to the spring well to give him. Again, and very importantly, there is no insistence by Synge upon the pattern of meaning that is being worked out on a symbolic level, but it is operative, all the more effectively because of its inevitability on a naturalistic level. The bread is the bread of life— "And it's destroyed he'll be going till dark night, and he after eating nothing since the sun went up"—on any level one may choose. And it is, further, the pathetic attempt of the cottage kitchen to comfort and sustain the riders to the sea—the hopeless attempt of the small world to reach into the large.

The holy water that Maurya sprinkles over Bartley's dead body and over Michael's clothes out of the sea invokes Christian symbolism placed in as ironic a context by the play as the presentation of the three Fates. The drops of holy water are themselves pathetic reminders of the implacable appetite of the waters of the sea and of the meaningless reassurance of the young priest that "the Almighty God won't leave her destitute with no son living." There are no sons left, and Maurya's turning of the empty cup "mouth downwards on the table" enforces the resignation of her words: "They're all gone now, and there isn't anything more the sea can do to me."

Water has become, in the course of the play, perversely identified with death, not with life or regeneration. Maurya's failure to give Bartley blessing and bread occurs by the spring well, the source of life-giving fresh water, as opposed to the life-depriving salt water of the sea, and the drops of holy water, within the context Synge has set for his play, become an ironic reminder of the frailty of human hopes. The desolation is reminiscent of the early scene Synge draws in *The Aran*

Islands, with the lonely stone crosses standing against the torrents of gray water, pitifully invoking "a prayer for the soul of the person they commemorated," but it is a desolation particularized, given embodiment upon the stage, even in the moment Maurya reaches out with her prayer to include humanity: "and may He have mercy on my soul, Nora, and on the soul of every one is left living in the world."

Synge weaves a pattern of poetic meaning into the colors he brings to his stage, both in the speech and in the setting of the play, as a part of the heightened effect of his play. Of these, red is the most effectively used, and the repetition of this color takes on the kind of implications that we have come to expect in poetry, where the interaction of sensory impressions is closer and more intense than one ordinarily expects in prose. The red mare that Bartley rides to his death is linked in the imagination not only with Revelation but also with the red sail in which Patch was brought home while Bartley was a child upon Maurya's lap (Bartley's body is, of course, brought home in a piece of sail). The identification of the color is given its most dramatically convincing statement in the red petticoats that the old women pull over their heads as they keen and sway for Bartley's death. Red is the color of blood, the color of sacrifice; here, the color of grief. Synge had noted in *The Aran Islands* that the red dresses of the women provided a joy unknown to anyone "who has not lived for weeks among these grey clouds and seas." The gray sea has triumphed, however, in *Riders to the Sea*; and the dresses become one more reminder of the frailty of humanity in its joys and in its sorrows.

Less insistent but equally operative are other color contexts. The white boards that stand on the stage from the opening of the curtain are fine ones bought for the making of Michael's coffin, and are pressed into service for Bartley's at the end of the play. And when the girls discuss the state of the sea by the white rocks, the audience is prepared for the identification of the color with death, for it is by the white rocks that Bartley will be drowned. Black is also consistently used in the play, perhaps more in its usual connotation than in the case of the other colors; for it is a "black" knot on the bundle of Michael's clothes (with the local meaning of *difficult* or *evil*), and as his body floated to the far north, there was no one to keen him but the sea birds, the "black hags that do be flying on the sea." There is nothing remarkable about Synge's use of black to suggest ideas of evil and death, but when Michael's grave rope is taken by Bartley to ride to the sea upon the mare, the prophetic implication is given particular color by the fact that the pig with black feet had been eating it—a pig destined itself for death and the jobber.

A recurrent pattern of superimposed events also widens the horizon of the play and establishes the sense of repetition, of the closing circle of death in the world of the play. In this function the figure of the drowned Michael dominates the opening of the play and persists as a presence among the characters. He is not only a part of Maurya's vision but also a reminder of the ruthlessness of the sea; he becomes *present* through the bundle of his clothing the priest has brought. "And isn't it a pitiful thing when there is nothing left of a man who was a great rower and fisher but a bit of an old shirt and a plain stocking?" His identity is established, but he is also a general symbol for all the drowned men of the sea: "There does be a power of young men floating round in the sea, and what way would they know if it was Michael they had, or another man like him, for when a man is nine days in the sea, and the wind blowing, it's hard set his own mother would be to say what man was in it." As the girls discover, Michael's shirt is worn by Bartley as he rides to his death, for his own had been that morning prophetically made "heavy with the salt in it." And it is a stick Michael has brought to the house that Maurya takes to lean on as she makes her painful journey to the spring well to give Bartley his bit of bread. This seems to Maurya a violation of the natural order ("In the big world the old people do be leaving things after them for their sons. . . ."), a violation that is natural—typical, at least—on the island, where the words of the priest are simply not relevant, based as they are on a vision of a world in which what is "natural" is also that which is just. "It's little the like of him knows of the sea."

The pattern of repetition builds in intensity as the play approaches its conclusion, for, in a wonderfully effective scene, Synge gives us Maurya telling of the deaths of all the men of the family. As she describes the neighbors bringing in Patch in "the half of a red sail, and water dripping out of it," Bartley, who had been then a baby lying on her knees, is carried in: "They're carrying a thing among them, and there's water dripping out of it and leaving a track by the big stones." Childhood to manhood to death: the cycle of life is fulfilled, and nothing remains but acceptance and cessation from struggle. Michael's coffin boards will do as well for Bartley. The only wonder is that Maurya has forgotten the coffin nails.

The neighbors who bring in Bartley's body move with sure familiarity, performing the necessary and familiar tasks; and with the keening women and the kneeling men, the sense of the community of death among the islanders is firmly established. The keen is a formalized expression of grief, pagan in origin, choral in function. By ritual, pagan and Christian, by formalizing grief, death is endured; and the conclusion of *Riders to the Sea* is reminiscent in many respects of the graveyard scenes of *The Aran Islands,* in which Christian prayer follows the keening for the dead: "There was an irony in these words of atonement and Catholic belief spoken by voices that were still hoarse with the cries of pagan desperation." Irony is not the right word to apply to the effect of the conclusion of *Riders to the Sea,* although for Synge it may have been present in the undifferentiated use of pagan and Christian ritual; the rituals are equally ineffectual in *changing* this universe, but they do enable human beings to endure it. The ritualized ending of the play has the effect of the formal coda of Greek or Renaissance drama, and it contributes to the sense of impersonal, "ritual" tragedy that marks this play.

Although Maurya is the central figure, the tragedy is nonetheless largely external in its presentation, objective in its lack of personal emphasis. The antagonist is the sea, an unseen but very real presence; and Maurya as protagonist is "like a type of the women's life on the islands" more than she is a personally realized character. Attention is focused upon Maurya from the beginning of the play; the speeches of the two girls, even before she appears, show a concern for her reactions rather than for their own. It is also her reaction to the death of Bartley rather than his death per se that is the (muted) surprise of the play, for she is able in the end of the play to answer her earlier question to Bartley: "What way will I live and the girls with me, and I an old woman looking for the grave?" Her conflict with Bartley, her attempt to keep him from going on the sea, points up the deeper conflict between the cottage and the sea, for "It's the life of a young man to be going on the sea," although as Maurya knows, death is the necessary outcome of such a life.

Mary King in *The Drama of J. M. Synge* reads this conflict in economic terms, seeing the basic conflict of the play as the "irresistible encroachment of a commodity-based society" that changes old relationships for new, so that the conflict between Maurya and Bartley has a different kind of inevitability about it.[3] Synge makes it clear in his book about the Aran Islands that he senses the impinging change that will take place as modern means of production and distribution come to the islands and the effect it will have on the last and most primitive place he knows, and there is also a strong sense in *The Aran Islands* that it is exactly this threat of mutability that gives a special poignancy to his work, but it is important to remember that the necessity of the islanders to face that ancient antagonist the sea is one that stretches far back to the beginnings of life on the islands and that Bartley, whatever the economic imperatives that drive him, is only, in the play, the last of the many men of the family who have been riders to the sea and have perished in the necessary and unequal contest. Whatever subtexts critics may find, in *Riders to the Sea* Synge admires the unpretentious heroism of these people and their struggle with the sea as a part of the natural cycle of their lives.

Poetry of the Theater

Part of Synge's achievement is to make the reader and the audience aware that the action of this brief moment of his play takes place on the last day of a long struggle—stretching literally over generations—that the mother has waged with the sea; and he has done this by creating an intensity that pushes back the limits imposed by the brevity of the play. The play moves with an intensity that can only be achieved by poetic means, and although *Riders to the Sea* is not technically poetic drama, it is one of the finest of twentieth-century examples of poetry of the theater (to be distinguished, in Cocteau's terms, from poetry *in* the theater). The rhythmic language of the play, while not in "verse" lines, adds to the total effect—much more powerfully, in fact, than the verse in many verse dramas. There is an appropriate austerity in the language and rhythmic speech of the characters, as well as an effective mingling of innocence and muted awe before the fate that has the family so firmly in its grasp. The speeches of Maurya—particularly the longer ones in the concluding moments of the play—have a formal quality as she recounts, almost ritualistically, the triumphs of fate and the losses of humankind.

A comparison of *Riders to the Sea* with *Blood Wedding,* a consciously poetic drama by the Spanish poet García Lorca, underscores the poetic nature of Synge's play. *Blood Wedding* invites comparison, for it is, like *Riders to the Sea,* a folk tragedy and a tragedy of fate. It is also, however, a play that, like *Riders to the Sea,* transcends its origin in folk tragedy to make a large universal statement. The situations are similar also; in both plays there is the death of a male line as the result of the unyielding demands of fate, although the Lorca play (written thirty years after

Riders to the Sea) is more complex and not so single in its effect as the Synge play, a complexity which is reflected in the multiplicity of theatrical techniques and poetic devices that Lorca uses in his tragedy of three acts and seven scenes. Yet the effect is the same as that of the one-act, one-scene play by Synge, and the conclusions of the two plays have a similar quality. In both plays the women endure; the necessary demands of life and manhood have caused the death of the men of the families in the irresistible working out of a struggle begun long before the opening curtain of either play. The neighbors are used in both plays to establish the community implications of the tragedies; and Lorca, who uses colors as persistently for symbolic meaning as Synge in *Riders to the Sea,* opens his final scene with two girls winding a red skein, an effect that makes the same comment as the similar symbolic elements in the Synge play.

Riders to the Sea is no more a static drama than is *Blood Wedding,* a notion that has persisted even in the opinion of John Gassner, one of the finest modern critics of drama. "The play is truly, profoundly 'static drama,' the theory for which was laid down by another 'symbolist' successor of Baudelaire, Verlaine, Rimbaud, and other *decadents,* Maurice Maeterlinck."[4] *Riders to the Sea,* according to Gassner, lacks the active engagement of the characters in their tragic fates that one finds, for example, in Sophocles' *Oedipus.* Synge was reading Maeterlinck, it is true, even during his first visit to the Aran Islands, and he wrote a review of *La Sagesse et la Destinée* for the *Daily Express* of Dublin in December of 1898 that indicated his interest in Maeterlinck. But later, in thinking aloud in his notebooks, Synge rejects the idea of drama that Maeterlinck represents: "There is always the poet's dream which makes itself a sort of world, where it is kept a dream. Is this possible on the stage? I think not. Maeterlinck, *Pelléas and Mélisande?* Is the drama as a beautiful thing a lost art? . . . For the present the only possible beauty in drama is peasant drama. For the future we must await the making of life beautiful again before we can have beautiful drama."[5] Synge is, of course, dealing here with beauty on the stage; but, as always, the reality necessary to true beauty is implicit, and he rejects the ideas behind Maeterlinck's kind of drama, which can exist only in the "poet's dream."

Synge's dislike of Yeats's *The Shadowy Waters,* which may well be described as "symbolist" or "static" drama, is expressed in correspondence with his friend, Stephen MacKenna,[6] roughly in the period of the staging of *Riders to the Sea*; and it seems most likely that Synge for one would have objected to a description of his play that would have placed it in the same category as *The Shadowy Waters.* In Yeats's play and in *Pelléas,* for example—plays which *are* "static drama"—there is indeed absence of the sense of active engagement; the effect is one of dream, of a fixed, unreal picture in which the playwright is concerned with the adornment of his scene rather than with its conflict.

Riders to the Sea gives an entirely different impression, although it is not possible to locate the action within the psychology of character, which is what Gassner seems to refer to when he compares *Riders to the Sea* with *Oedipus.* The conflict in Synge's play is a conflict with the sea, which is not, as in *The Shadowy Waters,* simply the element the characters drift upon. The sea is, instead, the antagonist—as unyielding as fate; indeed, it is the agent of fate in the play. The sea is not merely a part of a tapestrylike background as in *The Shadowy Waters*; it enters into the small cottage in every speech, in the clothes of the drowned man, in Maurya's fears for Bartley, and in every memory of the past, a past defined by the sea. A choice is made in the play that engages the will of the characters—the decision of Bartley to make his fateful journey upon the sea, a decision that is only a part of the larger choice made by all the men of the islands. And the women participate in this destiny and express their participation in the manner in which they face their engulfing enemy. The struggle between Maurya and Bartley is certainly not a static thing, and it becomes a microcosmic expression of the larger struggle—the contest between the cottage and the sea. There is also in the Synge play a strong sense of intensely real human *engagement,* of human commitment that exists on a level usually not the concern of symbolist drama. There are ways of behaving, rules for existence that are natural and confirm the dignity of human beings even if the contest with the sea is an uneven and a hopeless one. Although she cannot dissuade him from his going, Maurya's obligation to the unheeding Bartley is expressed in her painful journey to the spring well, bearing his bit of bread and a blessing. The fact that she is thwarted by her vision does not deny the sense of human obligation that is everywhere strongly expressed in the play—a play that is more nearly modern in its outlook and presentation than symbolist and more active than static, although the activity is not in accord with a modern preference for a psychologically centered activity.

Chapter Five
The Well of the Saints
Problems of Craft

The Well of the Saints was Synge's first attempt to master the three-act form, to create a drama requiring a different kind of control from that of the one-act play he had mastered with such relative ease. Synge had earlier worked at an expansion of *The Tinker's Wedding,* but in *The Well of the Saints* he tried to move toward mastery of an even longer form. Artistically, in spite of some delightful dialogue and an occasionally successful complication, both of these plays show structural and other weaknesses not ordinarily present in Synge's accomplishment.

The theme of *The Well of the Saints* is, however, one that looks forward to *The Playboy of the Western World,* Synge's next and his most successful three-act play. The power of the imagination to create and to destroy, and the compromises human beings make with reality, are the central concern of *The Well of the Saints.* But it would seem that in this play Synge comes closest to making one of the few compromises to be found anywhere in his work, for the play ends with a preference for a lie and an apparent insistence upon illusion. It would seem that Synge had accepted the dramatic implications of his material and the dramatic irony it provided, and these implications suggest a position that Synge had not taken elsewhere. Moreover, it is a position that the evidence of the notebooks and his other work would indicate that he could not seriously have accepted beyond his commitment to this particular dramatic situation. The only way to escape the implications of Synge's conclusion to *The Well of the Saints* is to read the conclusion as an ironic statement that, considering the alternatives, it is a matter of choosing between two lies—the illusion about reality that blindness affords and the figurative blindness of the sighted world and its social realities, which makes this sighted world unendurable for one who knows what literal blindness means and therefore comes with fresh insight to the soul-blind world of the sighted. Certainly this idea is suggested, but Synge never quite clarifies and strengthens the potential significance of this material. There are, however, a number of obvious attempts in the play to comment on meaning through the recurring metaphor of physical and spiritual blindness and sight.

One version of the play is titled *When the Blind See,* and this discarded title suggests what is the strongest social commentary in Synge's play, the shock of seeing the unsatisfactory life made by those characters who have had the advantage of all their faculties. Yet a comparison of Synge's play with *Oedipus Rex,* for which *When the Blind See* would be a telling title, indicates a marked divergence, for the Douls take on blindness as a mark of difference, a way of escaping responsibility for and communion with that which they have seen. They escape into a new fantasy about themselves as human beings that makes life possible for them but depends on surface appearances as completely as does the vision of the inhabitants of the sighted world. The irony is that the Douls are not marked by difference, and the acceptance of actual blindness is not a road to knowledge but a path by which to escape the human condition. This is perhaps only to say that Synge's play is farce and not tragedy, but as the drama develops, the audience is confused by being brought into sympathy with a choice that itself sheds little light. It may also simply say that Synge's sense of available choices marks him clearly as having a modernist vision in which there are no meaningful alternatives. If this is the case, *The Well of the Saints* fails to give its audience the kinds of markers—visual and linguistic—that would clarify Synge's vision in dramatic action.

It is, perhaps, Synge's failure to clarify through his dramaturgy all the implications of his play that accounts for some of its artistic weaknesses—most notably, for the absence of the dramatic compression and fusion of intention and situation that so mark his other dramatic works. In *The Well of the Saints* there is an unsuccessfully concealed attempt to manipulate the material, to wring from the scenes an intensity that the situation does not entirely possess. A failure of tension often results, and nowhere is this failure so evident as in the language of the play. The length of Synge's speeches, which had from his first play given the actors almost as much trouble as his rhythms, seemed in the beginning of the third act of *The Well of the Saints* nearly impossible, and in these long speeches there is not that sense of purpose that emerges in the sheer love of rhetoric in the world of *The Playboy,* a love of rhetoric that becomes an index and a key to the growth of Christy Mahon.

W. G. Fay, one of the principal actors and early directors of the

Abbey Theatre, recounts at length some of the problems the actors had with Synge's lines in *The Well of the Saints*:

> One technical trouble we had to overcome was that Synge had not yet acquired the art of breaking up his dialogue into short speeches, without which it is impossible for the actors to get pace. Many of his speeches were very long. They took a cruel lot of practice before we could get them spoken at a reasonably good pace and without at the same time losing the lovely lilt of his idiom. Take, for example, the Saint's speech at the end of the first act. "May the Lord—who has given you sight—send a little sense into your head the way it won't be—on you [*sic*] two selves you'll be looking," etc. Worse still for the actors is Martin's speech in Act III when he enters blind.[1]

The dialogue of the play is not the only problem, for the sense of padding—of a failure of dramatic compression and movement—is particularly present in the second act in which Synge explores Martin's disillusionment with humankind and his education in the ugliness of the human world. The failure to convince when dealing with this subject is almost unique in the Synge canon, and one suspects that it occurs because the material of the play failed wholly to engage the playwright.

The Well of the Saints, interestingly enough, is the only play of Synge's not to grow out of an immediate Irish source. The source for *The Well of the Saints* is identified by David Greene as Andrieu de la Vigne's fifteenth-century French farce, *Moralité de l'Aveugle et du Boiteux,*[2] but in many ways Yeats's *The Cat and the Moon* is closer to that farce than is Synge's creation. Other sources suggested for Synge's play include *Les Aveugles* of Maeterlinck; but, whatever the specific source may have been, Synge told several people, including Padraic Colum, that his play had been suggested by an early French farce. Only in this case, of all of Synge's plays, did the charge of a "foreign" source and influence have its basis in fact; but the intention of Synge's accusers, to demonstrate that Irish men and women did not behave like Synge's characters, was as always wide of the mark.

In examining what Synge made of his source, there is no point in laboring the failures of *The Well of the Saints* in dramatic execution; the play has its accomplishments, and these are of interest in the record of Synge's growth as an artist, a growth that made possible *The Playboy of the Western World*. *The Well of the Saints* examines a number of themes

with which Synge was to work in *The Playboy,* and prime among them
are the questions of the individual's conception of self and of the relationship of this conception to social reality. These questions Synge fails
to bring to a meaningful conclusion (dramatically or philosophically)
in *The Well of the Saints,* although an attempt to invest the play with
meaning by reading the role of Martin Doul as that of the artist in
relationship to reality and to society is made by Alan Price in his study,
Synge and Anglo-Irish Drama (1961).

In his generally excellent book Price is concerned with tracing the
idea of the "tension between dream and actuality" as a unifying theme
in all of Synge's work, a reading for which he has the precedence of
Yeats and of the early French critic of Synge, Maurice Bourgeois, who
claims that the "perpetual antagonism of Dream *versus* Reality is the
theme of all his [Synge's] dramatic writings."[3] This theme is more
obviously central to *The Well of the Saints* than to any of the other plays,
and Price's work with this play is probably his best. But Price falls
prey to that danger inherent in the critical tendency to seek some unified approach to the work of a given writer, for Price judges *The Well
of the Saints* as "perhaps Synge's most profound and sombre work." The
attempt to read a canon of work from a given point of view, to seek a
continuous rendering of a single theme or approach, often results in
this kind of failure of comparative critical judgment; that is, a work
becomes excellent for the preoccupied critic in proportion to its fulfillment of the critic's bias rather than in proportion to its artistic fulfillment on its own terms. For the concentrating critic, that work of
art is best that most embodies the critic's concern.

Worlds of Blindness

Synge's *The Well of the Saints* deals with two blind beggars, man and
wife, who have been convinced of their personal comeliness by the lies
of the sighted inhabitants of their small world, whose motives for what
would seem a kindly deception are called into question by the subsequent action of the play. A wandering saint, who carries holy water
from a distant, sacred well, heals the two beggars of their blindness.
The pair pathetically discover each other's physical ugliness and, subsequently, the deeper ugliness of the normal, "civilized" world of
sighted men. Martin Doul, who then leaves his wife, Mary, feels that
only the once-blind can have a true appreciation of beauty; and he
attempts to win over Molly Byrne, a lovely young woman who plays

with him and later shames him for his love just as his blindness returns. Martin and Mary Doul discover one another again in their renewed blindness and create a fiction that will make the future endurable: they may not be seemly to look at for the moment, but when age brings to Mary Doul the white hair that it inevitably will, she will be transformed into a beauty, and Martin Doul, not to be outdone, imagines that he will be equally transformed by the growth of "a beautiful, long, white, silken, streamy beard, you wouldn't see the like of in the eastern world." At this point the couple hear the sound of the saint's bell and attempt to hide themselves to keep their blindness intact. The saint's persuasion and the public pressure to submit to a second, permanent healing are hard to resist, but Martin Doul, with the keen hearing of the blind, is able to knock the can of sacred water from the saint's hands so that he and his wife may rest in their blindness for the remainder of their lives. The anger of the people for such ingratitude and stubbornness confirms Martin Doul in his decision to take himself and his wife southward, where they "won't know their bad looks or their villainy at all."

The play concludes with the procession to the church of the saint and the wedding party of Timmy the Smith and Molly Byrne, a conclusion that reinforces the isolation of the two beggars, who have rejected the ordinary world in favor of the more palatable world of the blind. They have entered a self-inflicted exile, but it is an exile made with a full awareness of the alternative. The ending of the play is not unlike that of *The Shadow of the Glen, The Playboy of the Western World, The Tinker's Wedding,* or even of *Deirdre of the Sorrows,* in which the characters, with full knowledge of what they leave behind, consciously reject the world of ordinary society and strike out on their own so that they may at least define the world for themselves, even if it is to be the world of the grave, as in *Deirdre.*

Much of the direction in Synge's development of his material grows in *The Well of the Saints,* as one would expect, out of the implications of sight and blindness. The blind pair have accepted from the sighted world an emphasis on physical appearance, on the fair-seeming surface of things. All their early talk is of the way they believe they look— fine yellow hair, a beautiful white skin—and when sight is given to them by the saint, Martin Doul naturally (and pathetically) identifies the beautiful Molly Byrne from the assembled spectators as his Mary. Told of his error, he successively chooses the next, slightly less beautiful woman, until he is brought face to face with the old and ugly woman who is his wife. The confrontation and the recognition of the pair take place amid the jeers and taunts of the crowd, who in their cruelty reveal their standards to be those same external ones they have foisted off on the blinded pair.

The saint warns Martin and Mary that when he has given them sight, they should not look on self "but on the splendour of the Spirit of God, you'll see an odd time shining out through the big hills, and steep streams falling to the sea." With sight, however, they attempt to become a part of ordinary humanity—a world that they find to be cruel and self-centered and one in which a beautiful face conceals a cruel heart. Perhaps the byplay that seems to be rather unnecessary stage business in the middle of this act may be Synge's attempt to establish the theme of the meaninglessness of outward appearance, for Molly Byrne dresses blind Martin in the saint's robe and cruelly teases him about his fine appearance.

The saint himself is a poor figure of a man, unattractive and frightening to the newly sighted eyes of the Douls. He seems to know little of the world, believing, to Molly Byrne's amusement, that the pretty young girls are the most innocent of creatures in God's universe. He speaks to the beauty of the natural world but is not of it: an awkward, uncertain creature, he sends his drops of precious water to the blind pair in the surer hands of Molly, who proceeds to mock not only Martin but also the saint as she plays stage manager with the saint's paraphernalia. The saint, although he has poor, bleeding feet and an ascetic mien, is nonetheless brother to the clergy Synge portrays elsewhere, for he is equally absolutist in his demands on the people, with no understanding of or responsibility for the damage his "wonderous" actions can cause in individual lives. He tells the Douls that blindness is a form of wickedness and advocates sight so that they may look upon the glory of God's world without the ability to see himself in it. Even as he pauses on the way to marry Molly and the smith, he would willingly separate the old blind couple by restoring sight to Mary, not understanding that only in their blindness do they have anything to share and that that sharing of illusion is all that makes life possible to them.

Synge suggests, but does not fully develop, the idea that the normal people of this world have themselves ceased to see it; they have become blinded by habit so that it is they who are truly blind, who do not see with the brief clarity of sight given to those with newly opened eyes not yet dulled by custom. Synge's comment about society is clear; even

Timmy the Smith, the kindest of all the villagers, is shown to partake of the values and limitations of this world. His relationship with Molly Byrne is to be built upon "a house with four rooms in it above on the hill," a foundation for marriage that recalls the situation of *The Shadow of the Glen*. Synge questions the quality of ordinary reality in *The Well of the Saints*, and he suggests a depth of experience possible for the blind, even if this sensitivity is necessarily built upon self-illusion.

All of the attention of the sighted world is turned selfishly inward, and Martin and Mary Doul easily become a part of this world. It is not until their blindness returns that they once again become a part of the outward world. With the sense of sight gone, they *see* the world about them in a way lost to the sighted world:

> Mary Doul.   There's the sound of one of them twittering yellow birds do be coming in the springtime from beyond the sea, and there'll be a fine warmth now in the sun, and a sweetness in the air, the way it'll be a grand thing to be sitting here quiet and easy, smelling the things growing up, and budding from the earth.
>
> Martin Doul.   I'm smelling the furze a while back sprouting on the hill, and if you'd hold your tongue you'd hear the lambs of Grianan, though it's near drowned their crying is with the full river making noises in the glen.
>
> Mary Doul.   [Listens] The lambs is bleating, surely, and there's cocks and laying hens making a fine stir a mile off on the face of the hill.

They live through all their senses except that self-centering one they have lost; and, with their regained awareness of the world around them and the vision that they now share, it is little wonder they refuse the saint the healing that would take this world from them again.

The world the Douls had made for themselves before the gift of sight from the saint was a kind of Edenic dream world in which they did not see themselves age, in which their shared acts of imagination gave them immunity from the mortal condition. The giving of sight brings about a fall into the world, one in which Martin is doomed to toil at the forge of Timmy the Smith, expelled into the world of toil as were Adam and Eve and their progeny. The pair had existed when blind by making lights from rushes, an ironic task considering their own inability to see light, but one in which they did not have to labor for others, working at ease in natural surroundings rather than slaving to feed a forge at which hard metal is worked.

The old couple, deprived by temporary sightedness of the harmless illusions that had sustained them, still have the wonderful saving grace of the imagination, and the third act is sustained by the blind pair's growing recovery of the autonomy of self. The act begins with Mary in despair at her returning blindness, a blackness that is blacker than it had been before the unhappy respite of sight, a darkness in which she can only think of her loneliness and herself as "an old woman with long white hair and it twisting from my brow." Synge finds the resolution to make a future possible for his characters by recalling an old man whose story he records in "The Vagrants of Wicklow" whose only concern upon his arrest is that his jailers had cut off his shoulder-length white hair, in which resided "all his pride and his half-conscious feeling for the dignity of his age." In her confrontation with Martin, now blind himself, Mary suddenly realizes the potential of white hair to redeem the disappointing face she has seen mirrored in pools of water, a face that "would be a great wonder when I'll have soft white hair falling around it." As the dialectic of the imagination takes hold of both of them, Martin, who has had only hard words for the old woman he has seen with his healed eyes, suddenly sees her differently. Synge's directions to the actor are that "*with real admiration*" he deliver Martin's retort, "You're a cute thinking woman, Mary Doul, and it's no lie." And then he can only ask her "would there be a whiteness the like of that coming upon me?" Her sarcastic response about his appearance, which includes baldness, calls up in desperation his vision of himself with something she can never have—a fine white beard that's "a grand thing on an old man." Their schism, created by external appearances, disappears as Mary answers, "Well, we're a great pair, surely, and it's great times we'll have yet, maybe, and great talking before we die." It is this promise the priest unwittingly seeks to destroy, and as the determined couple go to seek a new place away from the world they have seen with the world's eyes, they may perhaps be going toward hardship and death, but they are going as they have chosen. Much of the language of the play has been built around *blindness* and *sight, reality* and *lie,* and the end of the play suggests that only contextually and provisionally do those words have meaning.

Much of the dramatic irony of the play depends, of course, on the fact that the audience can see, before its eyes, the contrast between the ugly reality and the myth the blind beggars weave of their appearance.

The audience should also come, through participation in the activity of *seeing,* to look beneath the surface appearances of the villagers, to understand that their world is also one that is blind—built also upon lies—and that the choice the Douls finally make is not one between illusion and reality, but between illusions. The quality of the illusions provides the criterion for choice. Their gains in blindness are greater than their losses; their blindness is more honest than that of the self-deceiving sighted world. Nevertheless, their choice is one that denies the wholeness of the world, the totality of experience; it also denies what Synge himself had learned about reality.

Objections

Unfortunately, Synge never managed to bring the material of *The Well of the Saints* into a convincing dramatic focus. While the play occasionally finds its bitter voice, the playwright never succeeds in creating a sense of dramatic inevitability. Dublin audiences were quite right in objecting to *The Well of the Saints;* but, by and large, they did the right thing for the wrong reasons. The old claims of un-Irishness were raised, as well as the charge that Synge was caricaturing the Irish people. George Moore and others did speak well of the play from its first staging on (a fact that, in Moore's case, made Yeats a little nervous); and the translation of the play into German by Max Meyerfield furthered Synge's Continental reputation, although the performances of *Der Heilige Brunnen* in Berlin in January 1906 were not successful.[4]

Synge, in his last letter to Meyerfield, speaks of having "re-written" the third act of *The Well of the Saints* so as to "improve" it; but the revisions are minor and mainly exist to strengthen the dialogue. The weakness of the play is probably not of the kind to be corrected by improving dialogue. Frank O'Connor is correct in his suggestion that "in *The Well of the Saints* [Synge] invokes drastic dramatic machinery and then fails to exploit it."[5] Yet Synge's problems with the play probably have a deeper source, for it is never clear exactly why the machinery of the play was constructed in the first place. It is almost as if having become involved with the dramatic possibilities of the situation, Synge can find no conclusion that might justify the existence of his machinery. *The Well of the Saints* stands as a reminder of the totality of his dramatic achievement in his best plays, for neither the power of Synge's invention nor the considerable energies of his language can conceal or give meaning to the machinery of *The Well of the Saints.*

Chapter Six

The Tinker's Wedding:
By the Clergy First Invented

Not for Dublin

After the reaction caused by *The Well of the Saints,* there was no question in the minds of the directors of the Abbey Theatre about the impossibility of playing Synge's *The Tinker's Wedding* before a Dublin audience, and the play was not performed in Ireland during Synge's lifetime. Nevertheless, it was a play on which Synge had worked over a long period of years, its inception in 1902 making it contemporaneous with *Riders to the Sea* and *The Shadow of the Glen.* It was not until 1907, however, that Synge considered his play completed, and in a note to the preface he speaks of having "re-written" the play since the time he had worked on his trio of early plays.

Synge's preface, like that more famous one preceding *The Playboy of the Western World,* rather defensively attempts to do two things: (1) to point out the difference between his conception of drama and the popular, current drama of ideas (in other words, to help his audience with the apparently difficult problem of his *kind* of drama); and (2) to anticipate the criticism that his experience had taught him would arise out of his portrayal of the Irish country people.

Synge had not, however, as David Greene points out in his study of the play,[1] given to it the continuous revision that he gave to his three-act plays. The most extensive work seems to have been in the addition of a second act (actually the first act as we know it) to expand what had originally been a one-act play. The play shows Synge at work, attempting to move from the one-act play toward a longer form; and it also shows him in the process of eliminating essentially undramatic material in favor of the kind of concentration of intention and embodiment that the stage demands. The children of the tinkers, who are only mentioned in passing in the completed version of the play, entered more prominently into intermediate drafts of the play and were subsequently eliminated in favor of dramatic focus on the principals of the action.

The conflict between the priest as the representative of organized, authoritarian life and the tinkers and the freedom they represent is familiar material in the Synge canon. The instinctive natural life must ultimately flee the more sophisticated but quite meaningless repression of the civilized world. The conclusion symbolizes not only this conflict but also the fact that there is no lasting commerce possible between the two modes of existence: the tinkers take flight from the Latin mal-edictions shouted "in a loud ecclesiastical voice" by the priest who is determined to have the last word and who insists in this final action (as in everything) on the form and the letter, not the spirit, of the law.

The opposition of these different worlds is stated quite explicitly by Synge in two of the concluding speeches. Mary, Michael's mother, who is a delightful old rogue (and throughout the play the one consistent representative of the natural life), speaks to the priest: ". . . it's little need we ever had of the like of you to get us our bit to eat, and our bit to drink, and our time of love when we were young men and women, and were fine to look at." The priest's reply to his exclusion from natural and basic needs is a blow aimed at the superstitious dread of the tinkers—the residual gift of civilization. The priest fulfills the letter of his promise: "I've sworn not to call the hand of man upon your crimes to-day; but I haven't sworn I wouldn't call the fire of heaven from the hand of the Almighty God." As his Latin curses follow, scat-tering the tinkers, old Mary's judgment, "There's an old villain," seems fitting.

The tinkers come into contact with the priest because of the passing fancy of Sarah Casey to be officially married to Michael Byrne, the tinker with whom she has traveled many roads and many years and to whom she has borne a number of children in what, Synge shows us, has been a healthy and pleasant relationship over a long period of time.

It is a bit hard to understand the motivation for Sarah's sudden desire for marriage, although obsessive and absurd behavior is an ancient in-gredient of the comic mode, and the audience is not convinced by this sudden whim of Sarah, even when she says that she wishes to stop the evil insults of the respectable members of society. Nor is the explana-tion that her desire for marriage is simply a vagary of springtime sat-isfactory. If Synge wants, through a presentation of Sarah Casey's wish for a wedding as mere whim, to suggest that the sacrament of marriage has itself become merely external form, he again fails since the idea of marriage is, by definition, an alien form in the world of the tinkers.

What Synge is essentially after in his setting up of the wedding motif is approached best by what Northrop Frye calls "the mythos of Spring" as an explanation of the comic impulse—as, indeed, Synge's swerving away from the most basic traditional comic patterns outlined by Frye are equally enlightening by way of explaining Synge's comic genius and the difficulty it has given subsequent generations of critics. Synge's play has as a first alternative title, *Movements of May,* and at the beginning of act 1 we are reminded by Sarah that "the spring-time is a queer time," with its changing moon and season. According to Frye, the established comic formula that persists into the present involves the thwarted desire of a young man to have the woman of his desire and the subsequent resolution that allows the hero to remove the obstacle and to have his way. The formula involves a basic movement of comedy that "is usually a movement from one kind of society to another,"[2] and represents the triumph of the young and new (as befits the season) over the old. Synge has turned Sarah Casey's desire for a wedding into social commentary by skewing the formula in that Sarah wishes to join the dominant (old) society through marriage and the tinker (the title, we should notice is singular and not plural) is put in the position of acquiescing in order to have what he already has. That is, Sarah's true motivation seems to be to engineer a situation in which the tinker is forced once again to enact a perverse kind of courtship ritual as befits the demands of the spring season. He must make a ring and a marriage against his better judgment, or she will be off with Jaunting Jim.

As Frye observes, spring is traditionally the season of comedy, for the "green world charges the comedies with the symbolism of the victory of summer over winter": it is a time for the fertile world of ritual and the triumph of the new over the old.[3] Several recent critics have noted the carnival or May Day tradition to which the play belongs as well as the green man of folk tradition, which Synge made explicit in an earlier version, thus identifying the play with the roots of the Gawain materials.[4]

In Frye's schematic of the economy of comedy, the representative of the old may literally be aged but is primarily designated by rigid and repressive hegemonic views of the nature of social existence. The movement "from a society controlled by habit, ritual bondage, arbitrary law and the older characters to a society controlled by youth and pragmatic freedom is fundamentally, . . . a movement from illusion to reality. Illusion is whatever is fixed or definable, and reality is best understood as its negation."⁵

In *The Tinker's Wedding* Synge's priest, though not literally an old man, is clearly the representative of a restrictive social contract with ancient sanctions, and it is not accidental that as a representative of a ruling class he is first encountered coming from the house of the doctor, another professional dispenser, with whom he drinks and plays cards. Sarah, who does not have the sanction of living in a house at all, essentially challenges the priest's professional investment by asking him for the marriage sacrament, a place in the house of God, which he initially denies because they cannot meet his price. Sarah finally brings him around through womanly tears and flirtation, an act of persuasion that only old Mary Byrne seems to understand: "Let you be walking back here, Sarah Casey, and not be talking whisper-talk with the like of him," and she tries to call Sarah back to the world of the tinkers through the communal act of language by telling her a fine story "with great queens in it, making themselves matches from the start to the end." Mary's "grand story of the great queens of Ireland with white necks on them the like of Sarah Casey" proposes to restore for Sarah an imaginative order with the most ancient of sanctions, which does not need the intercession and restrictive rites of the church.

What the marriage ceremony is to the priest is another matter, for it *ought* properly to have a meaningful context for him. It is, however, as Synge prodigally demonstrates, a business matter for this particular priest, who seems, on a comic level, in every way to fulfill Milton's description of the bad shepherd:

> Enow of such, as for their bellies' sake,
> Creep, and intrude, and climb into the fold!
> Of other care they little reckoning make
> Than how to scramble at the shearer's feast,
> And shove away the worthy bidden guest.

The priest, who seems lacking in all humanity, drives a hard bargain for the price of the wedding ceremony: one that includes a newly finished tin can in addition to the money the tinkers have saved. The priesthood is a gloomy business responsibility for this man: "saying Mass with your mouth dry, and running east and west for a sick call maybe, and hearing the rural people again and they saying their sins. . . . It's a hard life," but a profitable and a comfortable one when the priest is free from his burdensome duties to spend his time "playing cards, or drinking a sup, or singing songs, until the dawn of the day." There is an ironic, comic appropriateness in the fact that, when the priest finally opens the tinker's sack expecting to find a tin can, he finds instead four empty porter bottles. And it surely is this kind of priest that Synge portrays in his comic poem, "Epitaph: *After reading Ronsard's lines from Rabelais*":

> If fruits are fed on any beast
> Let vine roots suck this parish priest,
> For while he lived, no summer sun
> Went up but he'd a bottle done,
> And in the starlight beer and stout
> Kept his waistcoat bulging out.
>
> Then Death that changes happy things
> Damned his soul to water springs.

Synge's picture of this priest is in itself sufficient reason why *The Tinker's Wedding* was not performed during his lifetime. The rough and disrespectful handling of the priest by the tinkers, in addition, would make this play impossible stage fare for Irish audiences; for the tinkers, once the priest has called out for the peelers (one kind of oppression calling for the aid of another), tie him in sacking and throw him in their ditch. The intolerance shown for *The Well of the Saints* would have turned to absolute outrage against *The Tinker's Wedding,* as the directors of the Abbey well knew. The material of the play would carry, for the Irish of Synge's time, an absolute and inviolable taboo. The word *shift,* which broke up the *Playboy* audience, would probably have gone completely unnoticed in *The Tinker's Wedding*: there was so much else to offend the Dublin playgoer.

Even the structure of the action itself refuses that normative, restorative function that has been a basic promise, even social function, of comedy through the ages, with the defeat of the old and the emergence of the new, a resolution of sorts in which, according to Frye, the "society emerging at the conclusion of comedy represents . . . a kind of moral norm, or pragmatically free society."[6] The priest as representative of the old repressive society is defeated and punished for his greed and, implicitly, his lust, for the tinkers have been able to reach him on one level by understanding that he is simply a human being carrying on the profession of dispensing spiritual goods, and their momentary, final triumph over him comes only in a violent, physical way. Sarah Casey, defeated by the character of the man who is the keeper of the sacrament of marriage, mocks him by putting the unused wedding ring on his finger to seal his vow not to call the peelers. The priest, the church, and the institution of marriage may have been challenged by Synge's comedy but no change has taken place in the society they represent and repress, and the tinkers leave, their world restored and perhaps reconfirmed only to that which it was the day before the onset of spring. There is no lasting commerce between the two worlds, no effect of the one upon the other in social terms. *The Tinker's Wedding* ends with all the tinkers crying out together "Run, run. Run for your lives," leaving the priest ironically *"master of the situation,"* by virtue of his Latin malediction. The priest, who has no missionary zeal for the saving of souls, has marked the separation of the two worlds by deciding that he won't have the tinkers coming in to soil his church. Instead of a wedding, a feast, a promise of new order based on a new understanding of moral norms, the characters, as always in Synge's comedies, leave the old world behind. Social orders fly apart, and the separation of the worlds in conflict at the end of Synge's comedies makes it clear that no meaningful dialectical resolution is possible. His vision of the world could not bend to a traditional happy ending for his comic plays. In an early draft of the preface for *The Tinker's Wedding* Synge writes that the play is "an attempt to catch some of the humour and freshness which is in all life, and which are the only food on which the mind can live healthly. It is a mistake altogether to say that [the] dramatist is to teach. . . . Teaching is always presumptuous, the position of the view of some fallible person."[7]

Synge and the Church

Yeats, as an example of Synge's inability to comprehend the political and social climate of Irish thought, tells in *J. M. Synge and the Ireland of his Time* of a scenario Synge brought to the Irish players in response to having been told that a play of the '98 Rebellion would be in demand. The result read, as Yeats says, "like a chapter out of Rabelais," in which two women, one Protestant and one Catholic, hide together in a cave, fearing to be ravished (according to religious identification) by the soldiers or by the rebels. In the cave they quarrel over religion, insulting one another, until at last "one woman goes out because she would sooner any fate than such wicked company."[8] Unfortunately for posterity but fortunately for Synge, who would have had another unperformable play on his hands, the company discouraged him from turning his scenario into drama.

In all probability Yeats was wrong about Synge's inability to comprehend the implications of his material. In fact, his persistent use of a recurrent conflict suggests that he knew very well what he was about, as well as the implications of his work. The quarrel between the Protestant and the Catholic women that drives one of them out of the safety of the cave into the unfriendly world suggests the absurdity of a rigid view of life as well as its dangers for natural human needs. In this respect, Synge's rebellion against "tyrannies on human kind" was based on firsthand knowledge, and it should not be regarded as growing out of the anti-Catholic bias some critics have insisted upon. According to Yeats's telling at least, the quarrel between Synge's Protestant and Catholic women is equally absurd on both sides, and it drives *one* of them out of the cave as the result of an absurd rigidity of mind, an intolerance bred of the religious attitude per se.

Synge was suspected, of course, of being anti-Catholic because he came from a militantly Protestant Ascendancy family, but the facts suggest that his intolerance for the repressions represented by religion came from his own encounters with the family brand of Protestantism. One example of this bias is the fact that it was the Protestant Ascendancy against which Synge aimed his mark when writing in his notebook at the conclusion to his first visit to Aran (with its almost totally Catholic population): "How much of Ireland was formerly like this [full of the free and primitive spirit of the islands], and how much of Ireland is today Anglicized and civilized and brutalized?"[9]

His dislike of repression of any kind and his lifelong desire for intellectual freedom were much wider things than critics who see Synge as anti-Catholic seem to understand. Synge's attitudes, without much company in the Ireland of his time, mark him as being one of the few minds of the Irish theater movement that might be identified as a liberal intelligence (in the nonpolitical sense). He was, it is true, a gradualist in political affairs, for he distrusted the quality of the passion he saw in the Young Ireland movement, but in his general outlook he maintained an objective, critical detachment that enabled him to question hypocrisy and middle-class morality in a way that drew blood.

His scene happened to be Ireland, and a concern with the Irish scene without a portrayal of the Catholic clergy is hardly conceivable, and certainly not realistic in expectation. The work of later playwrights, including that of Sean O'Casey, should indicate the inevitability of Synge's portrayals. In fact, in *The Plough and the Stars* O'Casey works with a scene between a Catholic and a Protestant woman not unlike that of Synge's that the company rejected; but O'Casey sheathes his final comment with a sentimental turn that Synge would not have tolerated.

T. R. Henn, in his introduction to the Methuen Junior Modern Classics Series publication of *The Playboy of the Western World,* states categorically in respect to the problem of Synge's relationship to Catholicism: "Let us be frank about it: Synge's satire is constantly directed, with greater or less point, against certain aspects of Roman Catholicism, as he saw it in the West of Ireland." This opinion of Henn's, although a fairly typical one, oversimplifies the intentions of Synge's satire. To agree to Henn's statement is to limit Synge's range in such a way as to invite the reader to miss the point of Synge's satire and to enjoin the narrow issues of Synge's early detractors. Synge's intention was to hold up to ridicule all that limits, all that seeks to bind humanity to rigid codes of conduct and behavior, and especially that rigidity of thought that makes possible the often hypocritical and unnatural modes of narrow conduct that he found everywhere in society. And Synge's scene provided him with the pervasive presence of the Catholic church just as certainly as it provided him with the shadows of the glen or the wild sea off the coast of Ireland.

Synge's treatment of the Catholic church in *The Aran Islands* is not unkind, and he shows his admiration for the courage of the priests who serve the needs of widely scattered parishioners, journeying through the rough seas in the same frail canoes that served the islanders. Synge's own friendship with the Aran priest and his sympathetic reading of Catholic religious writers suggest strongly that his stage attacks on the church were never merely the result of an anti-Catholic bias; rather, these attacks were aimed at a larger area of human experience in which the Catholic church inevitably played a part in Ireland. Often Synge focused his statement upon that aspect of humankind that invites tyranny, as in Shawn Keogh's emasculating dependence on the church's paternalism in *The Playboy of the Western World.* Perhaps, finally, what Synge did not understand was the limited capacity of his audiences for self-criticism: the anticlerical tolerance of the Continent did not pertain in a country in which the church had been the object of persecution until recent history.

The Tinker's Wedding focuses for many critics the problem of Synge's attitude toward the clergy because of the violence of the conflict in the play, but the excessive treatment of this conflict only reflects a failure of control in the play. In spite of his attempt to soften some of the offensiveness of his earlier versions, Synge feared a reaction to his play on religious grounds, as indeed he might, after his earlier experiences as an Irish playwright; and a working draft of the Preface to the play carried a specific apology to the clergy: "I do not think these country clergy, who have so much humour, and so much heroism when they face typhus or dangerous seas for the comfort of their people on the coasts of the west, will mind being laughed at for half an hour without malice, as the clergy in every Roman Catholic country were laughed at through the ages that had real religion."[10]

Synge's decision to delete this apology from the final preface results, perhaps, from a desire to avoid the already-evident tendency to focus on religious issues to the exclusion of the larger sources of comment and comedy. The paragraph with which he finally ended his preface is much wider in its implications: "In the greater part of Ireland, however, the whole people from the tinkers to the clergy, have still a life, and view of life, that are rich and genial and humorous. I do not think that these country people, who have so much humour themselves, will mind being laughed at without malice, as people in every country have been laughed at in their own comedies." Synge's decision to choose the more inclusive appeal for tolerance and good humor should be instructive to critics who read Synge as narrowly anti-Catholic in his views.

The figures of the tinkers themselves are not romanticized in the play. They represent the natural life, the vital and imaginative life; but they are nonetheless a cowardly, superstitious, thieving lot—a portrayal that should suggest that Synge is interested not in the presentation of opposite kinds or classes of people but in the dialectic of the opposing ways of life that his characters represent. It is only on the level of commerce or ceremony that the two worlds of the play meet; there is never any really meaningful interchange on the individual or human level. When Sarah Casey insists upon the ceremony of marriage, she imposes an unnatural difficulty on the world of the tinkers, nicely symbolized by Synge in the matter of the tin wedding ring, which is too tight for her finger and painful with its sharp edges. The making of the ring also involves the scalding of the tinker as he makes it, and the ring represents nothing but pain for the tinkers as they attempt to partake of the world of the priest, who is himself the final, unwilling recipient of the ring as a reminder of his promise not to inform.

The priest himself partakes of the tinkers' hospitality in an inverted gesture when the old "heathen" Mary gives him the cup of porter with the comment, "Aren't we all sinners, God help us!" and the priest accepts the cup with the salutation, "Well, here's to your good health and God forgive us all." In the sharing of the drink by the tinkers' fire the priest is partaking of a primitive sanction, a ritual commitment and bond older than the sacrament he denies to the tinkers. And it is one Mary remembers the next morning, when the priest has forgotten the spirit of his word: "Let you not be rough with him, Sarah Casey, and he after drinking his sup of porter with us at the fall of night." There is no communion possible between these two ways of life, however, no point at which to begin a real dialogue; and the conclusion is inevitable: dissolution of the interchange, curses, and terrified escape. Out of the dialectic has come no synthesis, no resolution. None is possible except in the perceiving and open minds of the ideal audience Synge never found.

Comedy: The "Instinct of Sanity"

It is interesting that Synge felt the necessity in 1907 of writing the only two prefaces he provided for his plays, a need that, in all probability, had grown out of his experiences with his audiences and the subsequent conviction that the plays could not make their own way in an unsympathetic climate of reception without some clarification of his intentions. In his preface to *The Tinker's Wedding* Synge makes it clear that he has no intention of writing a drama of ideas or a problem play. As in his other dramatic preface, Synge insists that "the drama, like the symphony, does not teach or prove anything," and he condemns both the "drugs of many seedy problems" and "the absinthe or vermouth of the last musical comedy" with which the playhouse of his day was too often being stocked.

The drama that he wished to offer as an alternative was a "serious" drama only "in the French sense of the word," not in its presentation of serious problems, but in the extent to which it would give "the nourishment, not very easy to define, on which our imaginations live."

A rich drama, according to Synge, will not be didactic in nature; it will, like "the best plays of Ben Jonson and Molière . . . no more go out of fashion than the blackberries on the hedges." The drama that Synge envisages, then, is one that concerns itself with basic aspects of the human personality in its relationship to the world about it, a more enduring subject matter than that of the contemporary "problems" that Synge obviously felt to be the province of the dramas of "Ibsen and the Germans."

The comedy of humors that Jonson represents—in which men are made ridiculous because of an excessive "humour"—and the inflated, rigid personality traits of Molière's comic figures are examples of the type of humor that Synge wishes to portray on the stage. This kind of humor he opposes to the laughter of Baudelaire, the "greatest sign of the Satanic element in man," a laughter that, for Synge, grows out of a poverty of spirit, a disappearance of that largesse of the imagination that made possible the healthy and health-giving humor of Jonson and Molière. Baudelaire's mind was morbid; therefore his conception of the nature of humor is morbid—a strange comment to come from the pen of the man constantly accused by his contemporaries of decadent, continental morbidity. In a section of his notebooks Synge further defines the humor he has in mind: "Humor is the test of morals, as no vice is humorous. Bestial is, in its very essence, opposed to the idea of humour. All decadence is opposed to true humour. The heartiness of real and frank laughter is a sign that cannot be mistaken that what we laugh at is not out of harmony with that instinct of sanity that we call by so many names."[11]

He felt, then, that a country that is by nature healthy and full of life will not mind being laughed at, will not object to a good-natured presentation of inflated portraits on the stage. What Synge does not provide, however, as a frame of reference for his presentation of such portraits on the stage is a sense of the norm against which comedy traditionally measures aberration. There is no restoring of social order in Synge's plays, no righting of the balance that nature and society demand. His particular view of the world and of society denied a sense of operating norm, something he had found only in the Aran Islands, in a special world, unsuited by nature to the demands of comedy.

The source for *The Tinker's Wedding* came, as Synge defensively stated, from real life; and a prefiguration of the play is recorded in *In Wicklow,* in which the habit among the tinkers of exchanging women is shown to be a springtime diversion. The central incident of *The Tinker's Wedding* is recorded at length by Synge in the same book. In the story as he heard it, Synge was told about a tinker and his woman who asked a priest if he would wed them for half a sovereign. "The priest said it was a poor price, but he'd wed them surely if they'd make him a tin can along with it. 'I will, faith,' said the tinker, 'and I'll come back when it's done.'" When the pair approach the priest three weeks later, they have no can to give the priest. "'Go on now,' says the priest. 'It's a pair of rogues and schemers you are, and I won't wed you at all.' They went off then, and they were never married to this day." Synge's portrayal of the priest is suggested by countless parallels in literature, including Chaucer's portrayal of his Friar, but a ready source was available to Synge in the *Religious Songs of Connacht*, translated by Douglas Hyde:

> Sure if you were dead to-morrow morning
> And I were to bring you to a priest tied up in a bag
> He would not read a mass for you without hand-money.

Synge's treatment of the tinkers is equivocal, for they are still the rogues of the original story Synge heard in Wicklow. But he gives us in the character of Mary Byrne the type associated in "The Vagrants of Wicklow" with the life of the imagination, much like the image of the tramp in *The Shadow of the Glen*. She has that imaginative sympathy that enables her to understand the limitations of the priest as well as other aspects of life she has not directly experienced. She is the one character in the play who expresses—as do all of Synge's sensitive, imaginative characters—the essential loneliness and shortness of human life and of the transitory nature of its pleasures. Left behind in the night by her son and Sarah Casey, Mary reasons: "Maybe the two of them have a good right to be walking out the little short while they'd be young; . . . it's a short while only till you die." She is also the best embodiment in the play of the natural life, and her songs suggest the oppression represented by civilization:

> And when he asked him what way he'd die,
>   And he hanging unrepented,
> "Begob," says Larry, "that's all in my eye,
>   By the clergy first invented."

The clergy and the law are linked in her song, which proves a prefiguration of the outcome of the action of the play and is a comment on its central conflict between the basic needs of human beings and those artificially imposed by custom, religious or social, in an attempt to control behavior.

In spite of Synge's familiar thematic preoccupation in *The Tinker's Wedding*, the dramatization of the materials of the play does not always rise above the level of farce. Even though the preface to this play carries a date that places Synge's final concern with it later in 1907 than *Playboy*, the material of *The Tinker's Wedding* remains in some respects transitional—a step in Synge's departure from the one-act form and an advance toward accomplishment of his longer works, in which plot itself becomes a part of the plays' dramatic life.

Chapter Seven

A Hard Birth: *The Playboy of the Western World*

Growth of the Play

Of all Synge's plays *The Playboy of the Western World* has called forth the most persistently uncomfortable reactions from audiences and critics alike, from the date of its first performance in the Abbey Theatre in 1907 to the present. Some of the underlying causes of the discomfort felt by audiences and readers alike have been explored by modern critics within the frameworks provided by Freud, Sir James Frazer, and other theorists. But the *whole* cause is to be explained only by an understanding of Synge's use of the dramatic dimensions and expectations of his material, for the reaction the play arouses is nearly always one of personal outrage, one not wholly to be explained by the Freudian contexts of the play. Reaction to the play differs from that the reader has, for example, to *Oedipus Rex* or to *The Brothers Karamazov,* the latter work, in particular, having many parallels with the material of *The Playboy of the Western World.*

Something different happens in Synge's play, and his success in affronting his readers' complacency in *The Playboy of the Western World* is to be explained both in terms of the material and of the play's artistic accomplishment, the skill with which Synge turns the dramatic mode into an instrument for the audience's recognition. The result of this fusion of method and material is the creation of the play that is generally acknowledged as Synge's masterpiece, at the same time that it is criticized for being an anticlimactic and gratuitously brutal masterpiece.

The story of the play, the core of which Synge heard in the Aran Islands, is deceptively simple. It involves the arrival of a young man—shy, footsore, and afraid—in an isolated country shebeen (public house) on the coast of Mayo. The information the young man is goaded into giving, that he has killed his father with a loy (a spade) while digging potatoes, takes on heroic trappings in the eyes of the countrymen; and, through their reception of him as a hero, the young man, Christy Mahon, is so transformed that when his father arrives, bloody but unbowed, he is quite ready to kill the old man a second and, if necessary, a third time. The inhabitants of the place are not willing to countenance the deed when it is performed in their own backyard, however, and Christy leaves, driving his father before him. Only Pegeen Mike, the girl whose heart Christy has won, has some sense of the desolation that must follow in a world that has been, however briefly, inhabited by such a playboy.

The care Synge took to make the material of his *Playboy* into a significant dramatic experience has been documented by David Greene, conclusions amply supported by the materials of the Oxford edition of the collected works, with the result that Synge's concern to control the artistic embodiment of his story is readily evident. Seven years of work went into the transformation of the Aran story into *The Playboy of the Western World,* and he produced at least "ten complete drafts of the play, each one written over and corrected until it had become almost illegible."[1] The third act, according to George Moore in *Hail and Farewell,* had been rewritten thirteen times.

An early sketch of the play that Synge had recorded in his notebook was called "The Murderer." Act 1, which was to be set in the potato garden, had for its principal action a description of Christy's life by his father, whose contemptuous telling so angered the young man that he hit his father with his loy and ran away. For this version, Synge intended to stage act 2 in a public house with Christy, in control of his audience, telling his boasting story, full of rant and great deeds. The third act was to climax in Christy's election to public office in spite of the appearance of the old man, himself as proud as his son of his broken head. Christy's reversion to cowardice is a significant part of the earlier conclusions of the play, with his deed surviving only in the world of the imagination and unrealized in any objective or meaningful way. Synge's changing conception of the meaning of his material is reflected in the successive working titles for the play, "The Fool of Farnham" and "Murder Will Out," which suggest realizations much more limited than that represented by Synge's final choice.

The earlier versions of the play and the changes that Synge made become an index by which his accomplishment may be measured. In the creation of *The Playboy of the Western World* Synge learned a great deal from the practical requirements of the small size of the Abbey Theatre stage, which could not accommodate his vision of a plowed field. Synge was faced with the necessity for shifting the scene of his play indoors, a move that underwrote the most important change in the final version. Instead of presenting the audience with the multiple scenes of the first version, Synge came to realize that the real scene of the play is, finally, Christy's imagination, just as the real action of the play is, finally, the growth of his conception of self. That the audience should see the occurrence in the plowed field through Christy's telling and through the reaction of his hearers brings what had originally been exposition into focus as an important and meaningful part of the action of the play. The unrelieved scene of the shebeen becomes itself an unstated motive for much that happens, and a continuous view of the interior of the country public house becomes a source of contrast and tension in the play as the audience sees the world of imagination at work upon the stage.

Synge's own comments about *The Playboy of the Western World* are very helpful in explaining what he was trying to do, although these are a part of his larger concern for the state of drama in his time. Actually, he left little behind him by way of explicit, formal dramatic criticism, except the two prefaces, each a brief but concise statement of Synge's intentions in his dramatic work. The preface to *The Playboy of the Western World* is a masterpiece of terse statement, the more remarkable for its contrast to the bountiful, sheer exuberance of speech in the play that it introduces.

In his preface Synge insists that he uses in the play the real speech of a real people he has known from firsthand experience. His insistence in this matter is partly in answer to those critics who had questioned the Anglo-Irish idiom of his earlier characters. Unfortunately, Synge's detailed account of learning to write the speech of the people by listening through a chink in the floor to the conversations of servant girls in a Wicklow kitchen brought new criticism upon the playwright and provided his enemies with the image of the prurient eavesdropper intruding upon the privacy of family servants.

Yet Synge's assertion of the existence of actual sources for the language of his characters was also, and more importantly, a corollary to his definition of art as "a collaboration." "All art is a collaboration" in the sense that the artist reflects the life of his time and place, for he gives substance and life to his work in terms of the world available to him. Therefore, a widespread loss of vitality in contemporary urban life seemed to Synge (as it did to Yeats) an ample explanation of the dreary work of Ibsen and Zola, in which the "reality of life" must be, by definition, dealt with "in joyless and pallid words." Given the modern urban situation, the only other possibility seemed to be an equally unsatisfactory literature; one that had divorced itself from "the profound and common interests of life"—the literature of the symbolists.

Synge as a "collaborator" in the Ireland of his time felt himself fortunate, for the language of the people was yet strong and imaginative: "in countries where the imagination of the people, and the language they use, is rich and living, it is possible for a writer to be rich and copious in his words, and at the same time to give the reality, which is the root of all poetry, in a comprehensive and natural form." A rich language, a living idiom, a fertile imagination are a part of the actuality of the world Synge portrays; and they make possible, by *The Playboy of the Western World,* his demand that "on the stage one must have reality, and one must have joy."

By *joy* Synge means life-espousing vitality, the assertion of the creative self, and expressive pleasure in speech and gesture to give form to the other two. And this "rich joy" can be "found only in what is superb and wild in reality." The attempt to present "reality" without "joy" in the theater of ideas or in the naturalistic theater of the 1890s seemed as much a failure to Synge as it did to Yeats, and both men knew themselves to be more fortunate than those "writers in places where the springtime of the local life has been forgotten, and the harvest is a memory only." This theater which Synge celebrates in his preface is one in which words and gestures of personality are of primary importance, in which the assertion of the creative self becomes the substance of the play, and one that shares with the Elizabethan stage a common source of vitality.

Growth of the Playboy

Synge's general theories in his preface provide an appropriate preparation for the play it precedes, for the discovery and the fulfillment of self on the part of the hero of *The Playboy of the Western World* are the principal actions of Synge's play. Christopher Mahon, the self-styled father-killer, creates himself to match the image held up for him by the excitement-starved imaginations of the country people, and the mirror itself becomes a metaphor for explaining what *happens* to the young man. The image of himself that Christy brings with him from the past was one reflected in "the divil's own mirror we had beyond, would twist a squint across an angel's brow." It is the image of the man repressed by the father, who is himself a raging "divil" of a man; and the image Christy sees in the father's mirror is that of "Mahon's looney," "the laughing joke of every female woman where the four baronies meet."

The shy, frightened Christy Mahon who first enters the shebeen of Michael James is closer in action and character to Shawn Keogh, his dramatic foil, than to the playboy he is to become. He is the son repressed by the father—like Shawn Keogh, who defers to Father Reilly and the church in all things and abandons manhood and its responsibilities in the face of danger: "I'd liefer live a bachelor, simmering in passions to the end of time, than face a lepping savage the like of him." The recognition of self involves the assumption of manhood, and although the instinctive blow with the loy is the action that has shattered the facts of the image of the past, it is not until Pegeen Mike and the others hold up the glass of imagination for Christy that he begins to grow into the image of self that is the logical consequence of the "death" of the father and the normal, now unstinted growth of the son. Although his action had been intuitive, Christy, as both he and his deed grow with each telling of the tale, comes to speak of the moment as an epiphany: "[Impressively.] With that the sun came out between the cloud and the hill, and it shining green in my face. 'God have mercy on your soul,' says he, lifting a scythe. 'Or on your own,' says I, raising the loy."

The old man, it might be worth noting, threatens Christy's youth with the traditional symbol of time and age, the scythe; and this is only one of the many symbols and metaphoric patterns that Synge develops in this play. Not the least of these is a rather extensive use of clothing in metaphorical terms, a use for which Synge has the sanction of a long tradition in literature. An example of the way in which the clothing metaphor works in the statement of *The Playboy* may be seen in Shawn Keogh's loss of his coat as he seeks to escape the duties of manhood, the defense of his betrothed in the first act. In the second act Shawn tries to bribe the playboy to abandon the field of sexual battle by offering him a fine suit of clothes, and Christy, in newfound arrogance, assumes Shawn Keogh's clothing as he usurps Shawn's prerogatives with Pegeen Mike.

The rage that had driven Christopher Mahon to strike out against his father had itself been the result of a threat to his manhood, for his father had wished to wed him to the Widow Casey, "A walking terror from beyond the hills, and she two score and five years," the woman who had suckled Christy as an infant. After the boy becomes the man, asserting and choosing for himself, capable of winning the hand of Pegeen Mike, his transformation is so complete that he becomes unrecognizable to his father: "That man marrying a decent and a moneyed girl? Is it mad yous are?" The contrast between the man who was and the man who is, is underlined with dramatic effectiveness in the interchanges in which old Mahon pictures the Christy he has known and the man he hears described in Mayo; old Mahon is simply unable to reconcile his early image of his son with that of the Playboy of the Western World. As Christy himself confides to Pegeen, "Up to the day I killed my father, there wasn't a person in Ireland knew the kind I was."

Equally effective (and more moving than comic) is Christy's own emerging recognition of self, which begins tentatively with the telling of his deed and its delighted reception by the people in the shebeen. It is Pegeen Mike, however, who appropriately gives him the image to which he commits himself, for she evokes his first delighted response, "Is it me?" when she speaks of him as a "fine, handsome, young fellow with a noble brow." The extent of Christy's recognition and fulfillment of the self's potential is acknowledged by a repetition of his question in the closing lines of the play. Old Mahon, recognizing the reversal that has taken place in their roles and that he must now play the heathen slave to his son's gallant captain, echoes with equal surprise his son's "Is it me?" The natural cycle has been fulfilled, for the father must give way before the son. The king is dead; long live the king.

The major action of the play, the recognition of self, demands the second "murder" of the old man by the son; but this element receives the almost unanimous censure of critics who regard it as anticlimatic, brutal, and prodigal. The second "murder" is necessary, however, as an index of Christy's transformation, for the first "murder" was intuitive and meaningless to him until it was reflected and magnified in the eyes of the people of the isolated public house. The import of the "murder" in the potato field has grown in Christy's imagination as he improves the event with each recital, beginning simply with the facts and moving, with encouragement, toward the creation of an epic deed of fully heroic proportions. As the man and poet sleeping within him are released, he begins to realize the implications that the deed suggests about its doer.

The Christy who has become the Playboy of the Western World at the games is momentarily thrown back into "shy terror" at the confrontation with his father in the last act of the play; but, upon discovering that he is as alone as every traditional hero must be at the moment of confrontation, he remembers the image of self that has been created and acts accordingly, thus giving objective existence to what had first found life only in the imagination. Although he had been completely subdued at the first sight of his father and willing, in the second act, to hide behind Widow Quin's skirts, his regression is brief in the last moments of the play; he recovers himself so that he may commit, in full consciousness and knowledge, the ritual deed upon which realization of self has been (falsely) founded. This time there will be no lie about burying the father among his spuds; fresh from his gory deed Christy intends to confront Pegeen, who will once again, he believes, give him "praises the same as in the hours gone by." He refuses now, literally and symbolically (in keeping with the pattern of meaning in the clothing metaphor in the play), to hide behind the petticoat the Widow Quin offers him as a disguise for escape. His manhood has been consciously asserted against the oppression of his father, and he will stand without disguise in the confidence of the fulfilled self.

The play takes another turn at this point, however, and Christy is forced to realize that in the eyes of Pegeen and the others "there's a great gap between a gallous story and a dirty deed." His isolation is complete now. "What did I want crawling forward to scorch my understanding at her flaming brow?" asks Christy upon Pegeen's rejection. Without the support of Pegeen, for whose approval he has struck his father a second time, Christy's image of self must fall or stand on its own merits; and the knowledge that the realized self is of inestimable and intrinsic value gives to Christy a strange exultation, which pervades his every speech in the conclusion of the play. This sense of exultation turns his first reaction of horror at the loss of Pegeen (who has failed to grow into his image of her) into victorious strength, and Synge's directions for Christy's words indicate that, although he is facing immediate torture and eventual hanging, he speaks gaily, delighted with himself. And when he sees his hardheaded father again, there is no longer a momentary fright: "Are you coming to be killed a third time?"

Christy's exultation partakes of that ordinarily associated with the tragic hero, and much in the play suggests the tragic instead of the comic pattern. The recognition of self, the acceptance of manhood and its responsibilities belong to recognizable patterns of tragic action. The comic pattern, which deflates, which neutralizes the inflated humor of the individual, is not observed in the play, except in the case of old Mahon, who is made to acknowledge the natural operation of the life process. It is not the main character who is made to conform to society, however; he fulfills himself, enacts the finally isolated drama of the heroic individual, and leaves behind him the unsatisfactory society of the Western World. The primary aspects of traditional comedy on the stage (which draws man as smaller than life, ridiculous in his pursuit of some inflated notion, and reconciled at last to the necessities of society) are not present in the end of the play, and Una Ellis-Fermor is quite right in her observation that the play is a kind of tragicomedy.[2]

As long as a great disparity exists between Christy and the image he and the countrymen create of the man "who killed his da," Synge exploits a wonderful and rich source for comedy—a traditional source, indeed, which rises out of the gap between what a man believes himself to be and what he is. This pure comedy finds its climax, symbolic and actual, in the games upon the sand. Christy Mahon, who has projected himself as a father killer of epic proportions, participates in games that parody the epic games of traditional heroes. He finds that the self created in imagination can triumph in actual contest; released by his vision, he is "astride the moon," "the young gaffer who'd capsize the stars." From his triumph comes the courage to speak to Pegeen Mike of love, and Christy has attained the penultimate stage of his growth. As the gap between the realized and the ideal begins to close, however, the play ceases to be recognizable comedy; and by the end of the play, the result is the kind of recognition usually reserved for tragedy, but one without the fatal consequences attendant upon the tragic genre. There is no death in the play except that of "Mahon's looney" and of Pegeen's brief hopes.

Knowledge comes not only to Christy Mahon, but at last also to Pegeen Mike, who has become the victim of her own failure of imagination. There is a tragic recognition in her final cry, "I've lost the only Playboy of the Western World." All the excitement of the playboy has made no change in the small world on the "wild coast of Mayo"; the transformation has been in the character of Christy Mahon, and his departure leaves only Pegeen Mike more painfully aware than ever of the poor and unaltered quality of the life before her, a life in which she had once been willing to accept Shawn Keogh as a good "bargain," there being none better. She has helped to create the playboy; but, confronted by deed instead of dream, she denies the man who fulfills the image she has held up to his delighted gaze. It is the poet she had loved and not the murderer, and she fails to realize that the one is released by the other, that the murder of the father is, paradoxically, a life-giving act. Pegeen Mike, who belongs to the limited and materialistic world of the shebeen, cannot follow Christy in all the implications of his blow against oppression. Her limitations are established in the opening scene in which she orders with evident relish the fine things for her wedding to Shawn Keogh; yet, when the prospective groom enters, she will not even look up from her work to see the man himself. Pegeen Mike is like Nora Burke at first, believing that a "good bargain" makes a good marriage. Shawn Keogh with all his property is an effective contrast to Christy Mahon, who has nothing to begin with but the possibilities of his imagination and the subsequent growth of self-realization. At the crucial moment, however, Pegeen is so firmly wedded to the world of Shawn Keogh that she abandons Christy and cannot hear his repeated plea to see him now as the man he has become and not the man who lied about burying his father in a faraway field.

One of the ironies of *The Playboy of the Western World* is that the playboy himself must quit "the Western World," having become so much more than the Playboy of the Western World; and a large part of this growth is symbolized by the release of the sleeping poet within Christy Mahon, who first discovers his poetic powers in the telling of his story of murder, in the elevation of a hero that he discovers, with something of surprise, to be himself. He is, as J. B. Yeats, the poet's father, observes, "a young poet in the supreme difficulty of getting born."[3] Christy fulfills his poet's role most clearly in his love duet with Pegeen Mike, who for all her lifelong habit of imagining a fine and brave life unlike the dullness she has known, is second best at fine talk with Christy Mahon, who would "feel a kind of pity for the Lord God of all ages sitting lonesome in his golden chair." The heart *is* a wonder, as Pegeen Mike discovers momentarily; it tames her sharp tongue, but, more important, it has created a man very different from the "quiet, simple poor fellow" Christy once had been. And the finality of the change is evidenced in the fact that Christy, at the close of the play, bound and rejected, is still the poet: "If I do lay my hands on you, it's the way you'll be at the fall of night, hanging as a scarecrow for the fowls of hell. Ah, you'll have a gallous jaunt I'm saying, coaching out through Limbo with my father's ghost." His imagination does not fail him, either, when he bites Shawn Keogh's leg (another action often critized as unnecessarily brutal). For, by so doing, he states in the only way available to him his refusal to become again the terrified man he had been at the opening of the play, and he takes a delight in mocking Shawn Keogh's perpetual terror in his contempt for a state he has now outgrown.

The power of this play grows, in part, out of the oedipal situation it invokes and the ritual murder it involves. The first "murder" of the father is not viewed with traditional revulsion by the other characters because, as one critic explains, it is akin to the ritual murder of the fairy tale, wherein the convention of the tale itself absolves the act of bloodletting of real horror; indeed, "the themes, the language, the import of the play resemble those of folk tale and myth."[4]

Another and an important element enters into an explanation of the attitude toward murder in the play. In a very real sense old Mahon "deserves" to die because he has sought, in his treatment of his son, to thwart the natural process, the cycle of growth and supersession of the father by the son. Pegeen's words to Christy that "it's near time a fine lad like you should have your good share of the earth" acknowledge Christy's right of assertion. Old Mahon's refusal to yield to necessity and to change violates the natural pattern of existence, the same pattern explored by Synge in the lives of the Aran Islanders. The old man is so intent on imposing his will upon life that he proposes to violate the most vital and meaningful natural pattern. Christy's father intends to wed his son to an ancient widow so that he may partake of the comforts of her home without assuming proper responsibility. He relegates his son to the level of a sexual surrogate; he intends to appropriate the use and fruits of Christy's manhood, and the initial rebellion in the boy is both natural and right, one that seeks to restore the proper order of nature. Christy's action has the sanction of a natural process enacted by ritual among primitive peoples, a ritual that may involve the actual death of the superseded priest or father-image.[5]

As Synge insisted to critics of *The Playboy of the Western World,* the story came to him as the record of a real event that he heard about in the Aran Islands, where he was told of "a Connaught man who killed his father with the blow of a spade when he was in passion, and then fled to this island and threw himself on the mercy of some of the natives." Sheltered from the police by the inhabitants of the island, the man was finally shipped to America; and although Synge's triumph in *Playboy* is in his own creation of the character and meaning of the man who killed his father, something of the attitude of the people toward the murder remains. The people can understand, according to *The Aran Islands*, a passionate action and its consequences; their reaction is the feeling of a primitive people "who are never criminals yet always capable of crime, that a man will not do wrong unless he is under the influence of a passion which is as irresponsible as a storm on the sea." Indeed, "Would any one kill his father if he was able to help it?"

Complications and Conventions

The horror of the people at the dispassionate second "killing" of the father in *The Playboy of the Western World* is a logical result of this attitude, and it is at this point that the complications in the making of Synge's play are drawn tight, not only on the level of plot but also on that of what is happening to the play itself. What might have been a play with a conventional happy ending—a wedding and a reconciliation—turns instead toward a deeper commitment, the implications of Christy Mahon's discovery of self. The necessity for the second "murder" is beyond the comprehension of the people of Mayo, who are— Synge would seem to say by his changing of the original geographical location of the story he heard in and about the Aran Islands—of the small landowning class, the class of Dan Burke, with all its limitations. The matter of conventional oppression is one the people can understand, and this is usually an oppression identified with the law (the rule of the English), as evidenced by the many references in the play to the "jailor and the turnkey" of Michael James's song: "There we lay bewailing / All in prison bound." Old Mahon's oppression is even more basic, however, than that of the English, for it is based upon the suppression of manhood and a violation of the sanctity of the personality. The Mayo countrymen can understand a reasoned blow against an abstract oppression like that represented by the peelers; they can even accept secondhand a blow against the father in a distant field, but a murder under their very eyes becomes another matter, and they bring all their righteousness to bear on what formerly they had praised.

J. B. Yeats in his essay "Synge and the Irish" claims that no one really believes Christy has murdered his father even the first time, that his hearers merely see before them a young man with a grand capacity for fantasy. Whether or not the Mayo men actually believe Christy is not of major importance, though, for their response to the second action would be the same in any case. Their reception of the first "murder" Christy reports to them is a response that belongs to the very conventions of the stage world of comedy, a world in which blood is never real blood and deserved blows never really hurt or maim. Instead, such blows become merely symbolic, devoid of any real sense of human suffering, for that kind of pain is not the business of comedy.

When Synge insists upon the "dirty deed" (convincingly reported by the ever-skeptical Philly), he turns his comment against the inhumanity of the hero-worshiping crowd in the shebeen, and, by implication, against the audience that becomes uncomfortably aware that it too has been willing to accept the murder of the father as long as it was distanced by the comfortable conventions of comedy. The inhuman, humanity-denying reactions to Christy's story of the murder have been precisely those always involved in the acceptance of sensationalism of any kind; and one of the paradoxes of the play lies in the fact that out of such a reaction could grow Christy's awareness of self, the most meaningful kind of human development.

When it is understood that Synge questions the comic mode itself, as indeed he does in all his "comedies," one part of the discomfort his plays have caused to critics and audiences alike is, perhaps, explained. This questioning of the assumptions that make the comic mode possible is Synge's intention in the scene in which Christy is tied to the table and burned by a glowing sod. This action, again, is not gratuitous brutality on Synge's part; instead, the torture of Christy becomes an action objectifying the cruelty latent in "normal" humanity. The people seek revenge on the playboy for having tricked them into believing in him (in fact, into creating him to believe in) and for having violated (comic) propriety in the enactment of patricide under their very noses. They have, of course, duped themselves in their inability to comprehend, in the first place, the human proportions of the deed Christy proclaims; and when, in his innocence, he strikes through the shallowness and hypocrisy of their hero worship, he has shown in them a failure of imaginative sympathy.

The cynicism that can be bred from convention—comic, social, or religious—is demonstrated by the general attitude toward death in the play. The conventional reaction to Kate Cassidy's death (whose burial was sanctified by six men from her wake "stretched out retching speechless on the holy stones") is a source of comment throughout the play. This attitude permits Michael James to berate Christy in mock anger not for killing his father but for depriving them of the opportunity for a wake (itself once a meaningful source of macabre humor):[6]

"aren't you a louty schemer to go burying your father unbeknownst when you'd a right to throw him on the crupper of a Kerry mule and drive him westwards, like holy Joseph in the days gone by, the way we could have given him a decent burial, and not have him rotting beyond, and not a Christian drinking a smart drop to the glory of his soul?" This cynicism is affronted, however, by the appearance of the old man and by the second "killing" by the son.

Christy is quite right in understanding that such a world must be left behind; he cannot free them by his actions, but he has succeeded, ironically with their help, in attaining freedom and manhood for himself. In the last scenes of the play, the torture scenes, and in Christy's departure, Synge dramatically questions the assumptions on which society and its conventions are founded. In this questioning lies part of Synge's originality, according to Vivian Mercier in his fine study of *The Irish Comic Tradition*:

Unlike the class-conscious Gaelic poets and satirists, Synge sympathizes with the underdog and the outcast, be he tramp or tinker, parricide or blind beggar. It is the respectable citizen who is exposed to ridicule in what William Empson would call the "mock-pastoral" genre represented by . . . [the comedies]. As Albert Cook has so brilliantly demonstrated in *The Dark Voyage and the Golden Mean,* most comic writing, the world over, takes the opposite position, siding with "normal" people and established society against the neurotic, the criminal, and the social outcast.[7]

It is also obvious that within the patterns codified by Northrop Frye Synge does not end his play with the wedding and the feast of reconciliation that comedy as a genre leads the audience to expect. Synge has, in fact, led us to expect such a resolution for Christy and Pegeen, one earned by Christy's domination of the games on the sand. What the reader and the audience discover with something of a shock is that Christy's true triumph is not as the champion of the games or suitor for the hand of Pegeen but rather as the champion of the inner self, a mastery that sends him away from the small world of Pegeen. The wake finally is the occasion that dominates the imagination of the shebeen, and the loss for Pegeen is as final as death.

Declan Kiberd, following the lead of T. R. Henn and others, examines the play as a mock-heroic parody of the Cuchulain cycles and concludes that whatever Synge's debt to the old myths may be, it is one that is discharged with total honesty of vision. The evocation of the heroic world in the society of the play can only lead to rejection of the playboy, for the debased modern world no longer provides the largeness of mind and heart for his dwelling place. What lives on in words without true emotional grounding is translated into a dirty deed. *Playboy* works its effects without compromise: the victory the audience hopes for both on the stage and for its own reassurance is denied, and Synge will not settle for a truce. When Christy outgrows and rejects the established society of the play, the audience experiences rejection also, for its expectations have been bonded to traditional ideas of the comic mode.

Christy Mahon takes with him the "joy" of which Synge speaks in his preface. His is a joy based on a capacity for feeling, for joining word and deed. It is the awakened joy of self-realization, which sends the hero out, as in all Synge's comedies, from the false world of conventional society—a world careful, safe, and materialistic, no longer big enough to contain the playboy in his full growth. This image of society that Synge created in his *Playboy of the Western World* was of lineament familiar enough to the playgoer to cause a shock of recognition from which Synge tears away, in his final act, the comforting cushioning of comic conventions. This shock, together with a web of political and religious causes, real and imaginary, created the "riots" that attended the play in its early years of stage life. (In an inflated gesture appropriate to the linguistic exaggerations of *Playboy* itself, the disorderly conduct of the Abbey Theatre audiences has gone into stage history under the title of the *Playboy Riots*.)

The Whole Issue

Synge, according to a letter written the morning after the riotous opening night to his fiancée, Molly Allgood (the actress Maire O'Neill), was not downhearted. He realized that the reaction of the audience proved beyond doubt that he had reached it: "It is better any day to have the row we had last night, than to have your play fizzling out in half-hearted applause." And, tired with the strain of chronic illness and the effort of his new play, he added: "I feel like old Maurya today. 'It's four fine plays I have, though it was a hard birth I had with everyone [*sic*] of them and they coming to the world.'"[8] This letter is not, it is well to note, one of a broken man, and it is not likely that in any specific way the disturbances attending the reception of *Playboy* or the unpopular reaction to the play had anything to do with hastening Synge's death as Lady Gregory suggested and as Yeats and the French critic Maurice Bourgeois seemed romantically inclined to believe. The facts are that, just as Keats died of tuberculosis and not of a reviewer's harsh words, so Synge died of cancer, not of the *Playboy* riots.

Yeats, who was acutely aware of the much-touted political implications of the *Playboy* riots, felt that the real causes for the reaction to the play cut much deeper than political loyalties and showed a world afraid of vitality, threatened by Synge's "joy." Envious of all that it feared to admit into existence, of that which it daily hedged against with the aid of social and religious convention, this world is portrayed in Yeats's lines "On Those That Hated *The Playboy of the Western World,* 1907":

> Once, when midnight smote the air,
> Eunuchs ran through Hell and met
> On every crowded street to stare
> Upon great Juan riding by:
> Even like these to rail and sweat
> Staring upon his sinewy thigh.

Yeats's poem, precise and accurate, is full of restraint when compared to an opening-night review in a Dublin newspaper, which called the play, among other things, an "unmitigated, protracted libel upon Irish peasant men and, worse still upon Irish peasant girlhood. . . . No adequate idea can be given of the barbarous jargon, the elaborate and incessant cursing of these repulsive creatures." The reaction to *The Playboy of the Western World* had not been unexpected by the directors of the Abbey, for their experience with *The Well of the Saints* and other plays had suggested, as Yeats had written to John Quinn in February of 1905, that there would be "a hard fight in Ireland before we get the right for every man to see the world in his own way." In this struggle, Yeats continued, "Synge is invaluable to us because he has that kind of intense narrow personality which necessarily raises the whole issue."

Although William Fay's claim in no way illumines Synge's accomplishment in *Playboy* and needs to be reconciled with the fact that Synge had already given years of careful work to this play, he states that Synge wrote *Playboy* in retaliation for an audience that had found *The Well of the Saints* offensive where no offense had been intended. "'Very well, then,' he [Synge] said to me bitterly one night, 'the next play I write I will make sure will annoy them.'"[9] Fay scented trouble when he first read *Playboy,* and with his brother Frank spoke to Synge and "begged him to make Pegeen a decent likeable country girl, which she might easily have been without injury to the play, and to take out the torture scene in the last act where the peasants burn Christy" (a request with which some directors and even the director of the film version of the play have complied). As a part of their argument, the Fays referred Synge to "the approved rules of the theatrical game—that, for example, while a note of comedy was admirable for heightening tragedy, the converse was not true."[10] The Fays were right in sensing what Synge had done in his play, but they were wrong in believing that the changes they wished could be made without doing violence to the whole. What Synge had done in *Playboy* was, in every case, intentional and not accidental.

William Fay, who watched the audience uneasily from the stage on opening night, 26 January 1907, has recorded that the first sign of distress followed the entrance of the Widow Quin, whom the audience disliked at once. Synge's implications that there are, in the eyes of society, murderers *and* murderers apparently hit its mark: the man who killed his "da" with the blow of a loy is heroic material; the woman who killed her husband by hitting "himself with a worn pick, and the rusted poison did corrode his blood the way he never overed it" has committed a "sneaky kind of murder did win small glory with the boys itself."

It was not the word *bloody* that broke up the audience as Fay had anticipated it would; it was "as irreproachable a word as there is in the English dictionary—the decent old-fashioned 'shift' for the traditional under-garment of a woman."[11] When Christy refuses the Widow Quin's offer of disguise and escape, he speaks the line that has become identified with the riots: "It's Pegeen I'm seeking only, and what'd I care if you brought me a drift of chosen females, standing in their shifts itself, maybe, from this place to the eastern world?" The play is, at this point, making its turn upon the comic mode, and the reasons the audience broke up at the word *shift* were probably a good deal more complex than the first-night audience could understand.

Out of all the bad temper surrounding the riots came a long, anonymous poem, "The Blushes of Ireland," which was printed in the *Dublin Evening Mail* and attributed to Susan Mitchell, A. E.'s secretary. It concludes:

We'll shriek—we'll faint—we won't be mute
    Until we've forced you to elimi-
nate that vile word, and substitute
    The chaster sh—mmy.

And, look, sir, do not sh--ft your scenes—
    There's scandal aided and abetted.
Let them now virtue intervenes
    Be chemisetted.

Yield Willie! else your day is done,
    Boyles will break out, and health desert you:
The little Fays your doors will shun
    In wounded virtue.

Irish playwright William Boyle did withdraw his plays from the Abbey company for a time; and, waving the "shift" as his battle flag, Arthur Griffith and Synge's other enemies carried on a newspaper attack full of venom. (The shift seemed particularly appropriate to the cause since it had been used some fifteen years earlier by Parnell's political enemies as the symbol of his adultery.) Audiences made it impossible for the actors on the stage to be heard during the first week's performances, but, although some of them agreed with the audience's verdict, the players courageously went through the motions of *Playboy,* saving their voices until the night might come when the play could have the hearing that it deserved. With the help of Yeats's speeches to the crowds and the protection of the police, the play ran for the week that had been scheduled, an action that Lady Gregory later described as "a definite fight for freedom from mob censorship."[12] The fight over *Playboy* was also carried on during the Abbey's tour of the United States in 1911, where riots and objections were raised by groups of Irish-Americans who had become, through their stereotyping of certain aspects of Irish character, almost that caricature, the "stage Irishman," the Abbey was dedicated to fighting. Fortunately, the lawyer John Quinn was numbered among Irish supporters in America, and he gave Lady Gregory and her troupe the help they needed in combating the ignorance and the uprooted but unchanged provincialism they met with in New York and in Philadelphia. It is interesting to note that forty years after the writing of *The Playboy of the Western World,* some of the American audiences of Eugene O'Neill's *A Moon for the Misbe-*

gotten walked out on the play for the same reason—they were of Irish descent.

George Bernard Shaw, himself something of a transplanted Irishman, took the opportunity of the American reaction to *Playboy* to speak out against the pseudo-Irish psychology involved: "There are not half a dozen real Irishmen in America outside that company of actors! . . . You don't suppose that all these Murphys and Doolans and Donovans and Farrells and Caseys and O'Connells who call themselves by romantic names like the Clan-na-Gael and the like are Irishmen! You know the sort of people I mean. They call Ireland the Old Country."[13] The stage Irishman whom the Irish-American seemed to prefer was in disrepute in Ireland at least: "the stage Irishman of the nineteenth century, generous, drunken, thriftless, with a joke always on his lips and a sentimental tear always in his eye."[14] The new Irishman may have rejected this picture, but he was sensitive in other directions. He felt that *The Playboy of the Western World* was a threat to the picture of responsible Irish manhood, capable of home rule and self-government.

Synge's refusal to trade an old stereotype for a new had struck deeply in the Irish consciousness, and the kind of truth that the play creates—one that not only avoids stereotypes but also turns against the stereotyped mode of creating reality—succeeds in challenging the reactions of all audiences, Irish or otherwise, and guarantees for the play a place in the history of the modern theater. "The outcry against *The Playboy*," according to Yeats in "A People's Theatre," "was an outcry against its style, against its way of seeing"—and Yeats's phrase, "its way of seeing" might well be used to identify what we recognize as a particularly "modern" interest of the stage in the twentieth century, as indeed it is of all the arts in our time.

Chapter Eight
Rare and Royal Names

> . . . it is not so much
> For disintegration of a lover or a kingdom
> Or burning of oak- and bronze-leaved
> Capitals that a queen grieves
> But that life, late or soon,
> Suddenly becomes, on the face, a jaded rouge.
> —Thomas Kinsella

Deirdre without Swords

Synge's *Deirdre of the Sorrows,* upon which he worked until his last days of life, is a sore temptation to the biographer and critic, for, in the circumstances surrounding the composition of this play, there are elements that nicely round out the romantic picture of a Synge who began his career as the *wander-vogel* of the Continent, only to be transformed into the full-grown genius of the Irish Renaissance by Yeats's magic, homeward command. The concluding act of Synge's own life seems to have prevented his last play until recent years from receiving the kind of attention it deserves as drama in its own right.

Synge was, at the time of his death, engaged to the actress Molly Allgood (Maire O'Neill), a woman many years his junior, who acted in his unfinished *Deirdre of the Sorrows* in its first performance in January 1910, from a posthumous script that she had helped Yeats and Lady Gregory assemble for the Abbey. That Synge, himself dying and in love, worked at a tragedy rich in its knowledge of death and doomed love is a fact to beguile the strongest critic. Unfounded legends such as the one Bourgeois and others (taking a comment of Yeats and exaggerating it) recount of Molly's acting out for Synge his *Deirdre* in the hospital room as he composed it each day[1] are innocent enough; the real injustice lies in the fact that because of such legends (and the truth, which is itself full enough of pathos and irony to need no help from unfounded tales), the play has often been ignored or approached from a biographical bias.

Two other factors that may account for a critical reluctance to take a long and serious look at *Deirdre of the Sorrows* on its own terms are that the play is unfinished and that it seems to be a departure for Synge: he turns for the first time to the Irish legendary material of the heroic cycles, which he had insistently avoided in his earlier work and had turned to parodic purposes in *The Playboy of the Western World*. He had condemned the possibility of making drama out of the "purely fantastic unmodern . . . ideal, breezy-springdayish Cuchullainoid [*sic*] etc." material that Stephen MacKenna had suggested to him in a letter that Synge had answered early in 1904. "No drama," Synge had replied, "can grow out of anything other than the fundamental realities of life which are never fantastic, are neither modern nor unmodern and, as I see them, rarely spring-dayish, or breezy or Cuchulainoid."[2] Synge's treatment of traditional material in his poem "Queens" bears out his reply to MacKenna; and there, among "All the rare and royal names / Wormy sheepskin yet retains," we find not only "Etain, Helen, Maeve, and Fand," but also "Golden Deirdre's tender hand."

A. E.'s *Deirdre,* perhaps the weakest and dreamiest of all the renderings of Deirdre's story to be dramatized for the Irish literary movement, was performed in 1904 with Synge's *Riders to the Sea.* A. E.'s play (1902), which reminded Yeats of wall decoration because of its total lack of living characters, was designed to be played through a thin gauze, hung between audience and stage to achieve the dreamy, misty atmosphere of a Maeterlinck play. Yeats himself reacted by creating his own *Deirdre* in 1906, choosing to concentrate his one act on the return and death of the lovers, managing to revitalize the ghosts of A. E.'s play, but ritualizing and formalizing the action at the moment of death. It remained for Synge to return to the complete story of that play of A. E.'s which had shared the stage with the first night of *Riders to the Sea* and to re-create the elements of the doomed fatality of human life that in *Riders to the Sea* Synge had so completely encompassed. The relationship of the two plays was clearly in Synge's mind, for he enters a parenthetical note to himself at the end of his scenario for *Deirdre of the Sorrows*: "death of Deirdre (Rider-like)."[3]

In taking the three-act form for his drama Synge directed his attention toward the human elements leading up to and determining the death of the lovers, making the tragedy turn upon the failure of human beings in the face of life's uncompromising demands instead of upon the betrayal of kings. And here, it would seem, lies the explanation of

Synge's choice of heroic material for his last play. Against the expectation of the heroic, Synge insists upon the nature of reality, of the human condition, and he achieves, through this contrasting material, a kind of dramatic tension that he had begun to learn about in his creation of *The Playboy of the Western World*. This is the same conflict as that which Synge's poems dealing with heroic Irish material always insist upon—the conflict between the "plumed and skinny shee" and "Red Dan Sally's ditch"—but in *Deirdre of the Sorrows* the outlines of the conflict are filled in with very human features.

Synge had considered at length in his notebook for 18 March 1907, the problem of dealing with historical drama in modern times. His conclusion was a predictable one: that modern prose idiom could not be put in the mouths of "antique persons," for the modern world is an unpoetical world, and to attempt to revive the poetry of the old legends is to revive an unreal world, to insist on the "poet's dream," which Synge's firm grasp on the nature of reality had led him to reject.

Synge's meditations about the problem of historical drama involved him in a consideration of the essential problem of the difficulty of creating poetic drama for the modern stage. The poetic drama, as he saw it, was also identified with the unreal; for people in the modern world could neither see nor speak poetically (with the fortunate exception of Irish peasants, whose language had retained a rhythmic and colorful speech). The "beautiful" drama seemed to belong to another world than that of reality. Synge concluded that the "drama of swords" had no place on the modern stage, for "few of us except soldiers have seen swords in use; to drag them out on the stage is babyish. They are so rusted for us with the associations of pseudo-antique fiction and drama." Swords, like poetic language, belong to the past. "For the present the only possible beauty in drama is peasant drama. For the future we must await the making of life beautiful again before we can have beautiful drama."[4] The problem Synge recognized is the problem of making drama whole, of making language and perception one with the material of the stage.

Synge did not abandon his ideas about the proper nature of and material for drama in his last play, despite an apparent contradiction between his theory and practice in the creation of *Deirdre of the Sorrows*. He had found Lady Gregory's retelling of "The Sons of Usnach" in her *Cuchulain of Muirthemne* (which he had reviewed for the *Speaker* in 1902) "charming" and had recommended it to Molly for her edification.[5]

Lady Gregory's Anglo-Irish rendering of the old tale provided Synge with his immediate source, but the play he created from it was far from "charming" in its emphasis. As Deirdre tells us at the end of the second act, "death should be a poor, untidy thing, though it's a queen that dies."

The story with which Synge worked is traditional in its outlines, related in its implications to the earlier material of Troy; to the later Tristan story, which is perhaps an adaptation of the Irish legend; and to the story of Diarmuid and Grania in the later Irish cycle. Given the almost overwhelmingly traditional history and nature of his material, Synge solved his problem of how to create from it by dealing with his characters as people, by choosing to stress all that was most human in them instead of all that was most traditional. He also chose to emphasize the unchanging nature of reality, the unyielding patterns of human life, which legendary material may express but should not conceal. Taking the legendary material itself and the expectations about human behavior that the traditional heroic cycles emphasized, Synge accomplished a dramatic tension by creating a vision of human reality at variance with the usual emphasis of the heroic material. It is in this accomplishment that Synge's *Deirdre of the Sorrows* is set apart from all other dramatic versions of the old story, including the operatic version of John Coulter in 1944, which is much closer in effect to A. E.'s creation than to Synge's.

In *The Playboy of the Western World* Synge had discovered the kinds of tension possible for the stage between the inflated language and outreaching imaginations of the characters and the sordid limitations of human beings. In *Playboy* his peasants in their grand flights of language talked like kings and queens and created in imagination a careless world in which a playboy could grow from within. This contrast Synge turned to a partially comic use by emphasizing the creative as well as destructive power of conceptions of human possibilities. In *Deirdre of the Sorrows* Synge has reversed his procedure. His kings and queens do not talk like peasants, as some critics have claimed; but their language is much subdued compared to that of *Playboy*. There is in *Deirdre* none of the conscious delight in the inflated picture of the world that we find, for example, in the speeches of Christy, comparing Pegeen to "the Lady Helen of Troy" or imagining the loneliness of God, who knows no such delights as those they will share in one another.

A New Kind of Tragedy

The language of *Deirdre* is relatively simple; certainly it is more restrained than in Synge's other plays. The people are simple in spite of their royal lineage, and, since Synge's intention is to stress the fact that their tragedy is that of human beings rather than of ancient kings, the use of common, serviceable language underwrites the total effect of the play. The language, which might have separated and mythicized the characters of the play into a special world, serves instead to remind us of the common humanity of kings and to bring home the pathos of the very human situation.

In *Deirdre,* instead of inflation of language and imagination, Synge takes the colorful, heroic legend and insists upon the mortal limitations of the people involved: upon the way in which, having been committed to heroic action, the characters find themselves betrayed by their human frailties, a betrayal that does not deny their heroic actions but does deny the possibility of heroic action that is meaningful in the face of individual life and reality. The whole of Synge's play about the pitiful condition of human life is set against the ever-present legend of great and tragic possibilities. His intention is to create a new kind of tragedy, one that denies the traditional, unreal material of the past while it affirms Synge's view of the grim nature of reality.

In a letter to John Quinn, Synge speaks of his consciousness of the problem raised by the material of *Deirdre of the Sorrows*: "I am not sure yet whether I shall be able to make a satisfactory play out of it. These saga people, when one comes to deal with them, seem very remote; one does not know what they thought or what they are or where they went to sleep, so one is apt to fall into rhetoric."[6]

It is undoubtedly a part of his attempt to underline the human qualities of the tragedy of *Deirdre of the Sorrows* that caused Synge to forego the traditional and dramatically tempting chess game that the legend provides and of which Yeats made such effective use in his *Deirdre*. In the versions of the Deirdre story in which the two lovers sit, playing chess as they wait for their certain deaths, one has a sense of the overwhelming helplessness of characters who are pawns of the gods. This kind of emphasis on fatality inevitably results from the simile-making game of chess, even if, doomed to death, they are also engaged in active warfare against defeat as in Lady Gregory's *Cuchulain of Muirthemne* or in James Stephens's later version of *Deirdre*. Synge's people are not doomed in the usual sense by the working out of chance or by overriding, universal fate; instead, they are defeated from within, by what is frail and pitiful in all human beings—terror before the demands of life, death, and the end of love and youth.

Synge has achieved in a single line of development what Yeats had attempted to do with a double plot in his earlier *On Baile's Strand* (1904), a play that Synge knew and from which he undoubtedly learned a great deal about the possibilities for the treatment of traditional Irish material. Yeats, in his play, sets up a tension between two worlds—that of the high king and Cuchulain, the legendary heroes, and that of comic reality, the world of the Blind Man and the Fool. With the two levels of his play commenting on each other, Yeats suggests the possibility of qualifying the heroic material by the intrusion of the commonplace world, but his qualification remains a formal matter in *On Baile's Strand,* of a different order from the internal coherence that Synge's *Deirdre* achieves. Deirdre and her Naisi find that they are doomed as human beings in spite of the world's insistence that they are kings and queens, and in their discovery Synge has created a moving drama out of heroic stuff, without dishonor to his own beliefs. He has made a play that answers in the negative his question, "Is the drama as a beautiful thing a lost art?"

On the Ridge of the World

Deirdre of the Sorrows is, like *Riders to the Sea,* the working out of a foreknown tragedy, the story of the irresistible and natural love between Deirdre and Naisi, which brings their pursuit, betrayal, and death at the hands of Conchubor, the high king of Ulster, who had reared Deirdre to be his bride, in spite of his knowledge of the prophecy of destruction that must follow in her wake. Her name itself means *the troubler, alarm,* or *sorrow.* Sorrow comes ultimately, however, not in the death of the lovers as in the heroic cycle, nor in the subsequent battles of the Ulstermen, but from the knowledge the lovers come to on the edge of the grave about the nature of human love and life. Synge, therefore, provides a reversal of the expected working out of the traditional material, which is itself foreknown but which, in its general outlines, forgets to remember the bitter truths of which Synge reminds his audience when they least expect to be made to remember them. The play takes the same kind of turn against the audience's expectations that *Playboy* does, but, in this case, the result is to heighten the tragic effect by increasing the audience's knowledge of the real nature of the tragedy of the world. The audience of *Deirdre of the Sorrows* responds with surprise, like the audience of *Playboy,* but without, in this case, anger at what it has been made to learn.

Synge begins his play with the moment preceding Deirdre's recognition of her role, the last moment of her wild and free childhood, which she puts off as she puts on queenly robes for her appearance before Naisi. In this opening act many issues are enjoined, and in spite of the fact that the play as we have it was not finished by Synge, a great deal of work had gone into it, as David Greene's statement that there are over twenty complete drafts of the play suggests.[7] However incomplete the first act may be, it is already a masterful presentation of the issues of the play, its setting of the scene, and its drawing of the conflicts and their implications.

The prophecy of the fatality of Deirdre's life is a part of the awareness against which the action of the first act moves. Not only is it present in the speech of all the characters, but the tapestry at which Lavarcham and Deirdre work operates with the same force as the spinning wheel in *Riders to the Sea*—to remind the audience that a destiny is being woven on the stage. The implications of the scene that Deirdre works on her frame are clear when she tells Conchubor that it is of "three young men and they chasing in the green gap of a wood." Naisi and his brothers are being woven into her tapestry just as they are to be woven into her destiny and into that of Ireland.

The conflict between Deirdre and Conchubor is a familiar one in Synge's work; it had been the concern of *The Shadow of the Glen,* Synge's first staged play, and later of *The Playboy of the Western World,* and is convincing evidence that Deirdre is not a departure for Synge but rather a continuation of his seven years' work. Deirdre's love for Naisi is a natural thing set in opposition to Conchubor's desire to make her the consort of an aging man. In imagery, the natural world is itself placed against the artificial finery Conchubor provides for Deirdre. He brings her "rings and jewels from Emain Macha" in contrast to the "bag of nuts, and twigs" she gathers in the hills. The attempt to thwart the natural is always a source of pain in Synge's work, and Conchubor's attempt to influence Deirdre to yield her natural impulses before the hollow promise of material security must have had a familiar ring to those of the Abbey audience who had been present for *The Shadow of the Glen* some seven years earlier. Conchubor, much like Yeats's High King in his conflict with Cuchulain in *On Baile's Strand,* insists to

Deirdre that "What we all need is a place is safe and splendid, and it's that you'll get in Emain."

The conflict between the natural and the imposed will, between the joy of the world and material security is cause enough for Lavarcham to know, without the aid of prophecy, the troubles that are coming: "if there were no warnings that told about her you'd see troubles coming when an old king is taking her, and she without a thought but for her beauty and to be straying the hills." The conflict is one basic to human experience, and it is reflected in the fact that Deirdre has had Conchubor's riches put away for safekeeping for fear of soiling them in the course of the natural, daily life, "running out and in with mud and grasses on her feet." Conchubor senses the threat to his world from the natural life of Deirdre, but Lavarcham insists that the natural life is right, that Deirdre is in her proper element among "flowers or nuts, or sticks itself," and that "so long as she's gathering new life" there is no cause for concern. The growing natural world prepares Deirdre, however, as Conchubor guesses it will, to reject that fixed and settled, artificially beautiful world that he offers her for her kingdom.

Much of the imagery and symbolism that Synge chooses for his play is resonant of pagan mythology as it is described for us in works such as Robert Graves's *The White Goddess,* and these images reinforce the relationship between the materials of *Deirdre* and the natural order, which is expressed by pagan rituals. These are symbols that identify women with the forces of nature; "[their] work as gardeners, keepers of the hearth and bearers of new life attuned them deeply to the energies of the earth."[8] The play centers on a female character, one of Synge's many dominant women characters, and the roles of all the women in the play are enriched by motifs drawn from pagan mythology, in which women as keepers of the natural are closely bound to the life cycle as well as being natural agents of fate. It is possible to see the three women who dominate the first act as linked to the Triple Goddess, or Moon Goddess, representing the phases of the moon from the crescent (Deirdre or the young virgin) to full or mature (Lavarcham) and finally to the dark (the old woman). "Hidden away in a wood, the women embody the forces at work behind the life of appearances."[9]

The first act opens with Lavarcham working at a tapestry that is in Deirdre's design and colors. Her anxiety about Deirdre's not having returned by the time evening arrives is heightened when the old woman tells her that the sons of Usna are nearby, for they have been "chasing hares for two days or three, and the same a while since when the moon was full." The hunters are approaching the domain of the Triple Goddess, whose sacred number is three, whose symbolic animal is the hare, with its triangular teeth, its litters of three, its swiftness and fertility; some identify it with the moon, which is said to show the image of the hare on its face. The approach of Naisi and his brothers signals the beginning of the working out of the prophecy.

When Deirdre dresses herself as a queen to receive Naisi, after having met Conchubar in clothes that were dirty and unkempt from her day in the hills, she evokes the pagan rite of the sacred marriage by which the woman chooses her husband and initiates him into the special wisdom of nature, and it is important to notice that it is Deirdre who is responsible for Naisi's coming to the house in the wood. When she defiantly tells Conchubor that "A girl born, the way I'm born, is more likely to wish for a mate who'd be her likeness . . . a man with his hair like the raven maybe and his skin like the snow and his lips like the blood spilt on it," she has already seen Naisi, told him where to find her, and chosen to accept her fate. The subject of her tapestry, she tells Conchubor, is of "three young men, and they chasing in the green gap of a wood." When he offers her instead white hounds with silver chains and the finest gray horses, Synge makes it clear that they represent different worlds and will remain forever worlds apart.

Naisi and his brothers are always identified with the natural world; they are hunters who "have no match and they chasing in the woods." Like Deirdre they belong to the woods, and all of nature is invoked in recognition of the natural union of the two lovers: "By the sun and moon and the whole earth, I wed Deirdre to Naisi. May the air bless you, and water and the wind, the sea, and all the hours of the sun and moon." The lines of the conflict between the two worlds are quickly and clearly drawn in this first act, and if Synge had rested here, the play *might* have been the simple play Ellis-Fermor labels it in *The Irish Dramatic Movement*.

Deirdre of the Sorrows is not simple, however, and the first act lays the dramatic groundwork for all the action that is to come. Conchubor, as a representative of that world that attempts to mold life to preconceived patterns, has tried to create of Deirdre's natural beauty his conception of his proper consort. He even believes that he can thwart the destiny foretold by prophecy at her birth: "It is I will be your comrade and will stand between you and the great troubles are foretold." Like

Oedipus, Conchubor believes that he can make his destiny, not knowing that he hastens it at the moment he insists on taking Deirdre into
the "safety" of his protection.

In spite of this (unfulfillable) promise of a long and comfortable
queenly life, Deirdre follows her natural desires; and Lavarcham, who
speaks with choral and prophetic voice, acknowledges that "she's as
good a right as another, maybe, having her pleasure, though she'd spoil
the world." Deirdre, who accepts the inevitability of the prophecy,
knows that her pleasure will be brief: "It should be a sweet thing to
have what is best and richest, if it's for a short space only." She makes
her choice, but beyond the knowledge her choice involves, there is
another truth that she knows, although the knowledge will not help
deaden her pain when the actuality rises to confront her in the later
acts of the play: "Isn't it a small thing is foretold about the ruin of
ourselves, Naisi, when all men have age coming and great ruin in the
end." The sense is strong in Deirdre of the doomed mortality of all
men—a truth that makes small the specific ruin foretold in this tale of
kings. Her knowledge, a part of that natural response to life, is so
strong in her that it prepares for her acceptance of age and death as a
part of the whole; there is in her none of Conchubor's attempt to impose his own rule on life, to deny his age with a young bride.

The first act takes place under the shadow of a storm, which symbolizes and foretells the inevitable tragedy of the play. We are told in
the opening lines that the scene is dark with the clouds that are gathering, and it is Deirdre's knowledge of the coming storm that brings
Naisi and his brothers to find her in Lavarcham's house on Slieve
Fuadh. The storm, which Synge perhaps borrowed from his continual
reading of Shakespeare, externalizes the conflicts that are brought to a
head in the scene and dramatizes the moment for the characters' acceptance of the full responsibility of identity. As William Empson observes
of the storm, "on the classical tragic model it makes the day of the
action an unusual one, a day on which it seems fitting that great things
should happen."[10] Deirdre takes on the queenly robes suitable to the
role she is destined to enact and she identifies herself to the sons of
Usna in a line that recalls Hamlet's recognition line, "This is I, Hamlet
the Dane." Standing in the doorway, on the threshold of her new life,
she calls, "Naisi! Do not leave me, Naisi. I am Deirdre of the Sorrows."
The storm that has driven Conchubor early back to Emain Macha has
brought Naisi to Deirdre and Deirdre to her destiny. As the storm

clears, a sense of calm acceptance of inevitable tragedy concludes the act with an invocation of nature to bless this union of lovers. Lavarcham's comment recognizes the natural sanction of this marriage in the face of doom: "Isn't it a hard thing you're doing, but who can help it? Birds go mating in the spring of the year, and ewes at the leaves falling, but a young girl must have her lover in all the course of the sun and moon."

The second act, which seems the least finished of the three, is set in Scotland, seven years after Deirdre and the sons of Usna have fled Ulster and the court. Fergus has come from Conchubor as surety for safe conduct if Deirdre and the three brothers will return to Ireland, and Synge is faced with the problem of creating a pivotal statement to prepare for the tragic consequences that will close the drama. The act as it stands suggests that Synge was working with an overplus of ideas and motivations, for there is not here—as in the first and last acts— that sense of dramatic certainty and necessity that is typical of Synge's completed plays.

The Deirdre of the second act is a woman resigned to fate, almost wearily ready for it. Her seven fair-seeming years with Naisi have been marked by a daily dread of the next day's loss. It has not been wholly "a sweet thing," having "what is best and richest, if it's for a short space only," for the Deirdre of this act has been "wondering all times is it a game worth playing, living on until you're dried and old, and our joy is gone for ever." She has resigned herself at the sight of Fergus on the shore to the conclusion of their fated course; and, although Synge has made her from the beginning a woman rich in knowledge of the whole demands of life, she seems in this act almost eager to have done with it, an attitude for which Synge has not properly prepared the audience.

The character of Owen is briefly introduced in act 2, perhaps as a way of motivating Deirdre's attitude; but, in the play as it stands now, he comes after she has already revealed her weariness with life. His appearance is at best contrived, for he has been sent as Conchubor's spy and yet comes out of love for Deirdre. He has been hiding three weeks in the bog, waiting a chance to speak to Deirdre alone, and after two brief appearances he goes out to his suicide, unable to endure a world in which Deirdre stubbornly accepts inevitable death, although she does so, in part, in response to what he has told her. The whole business with Owen is roughly managed, something which Synge had obviously not concluded; for shortly before his death, Synge spoke to Yeats about a "grotesque" character he had added to the second act, who had yet to be woven into act 1.[11]

Owen is the wise fool of Renaissance drama, who speaks in excesses and in riddles, yet makes consummate sense. Upon her decision to stay with Naisi wherever he may go, Owen tells Deirdre (as if she were not already intensely aware of it) that "Queens get old . . . with their white and long arms going from them, and their backs hooping." And the answer to his riddle of why his father isn't as old and ugly as Conchubor is that Naisi had killed him before he had a chance to age. Lavarcham, who had been a lover of Owen's father, is held up before Deirdre as an example of the way she will someday appear to Naisi. Owen is an Elizabethan character who has wandered into Synge's play and been made, temporarily at least, welcome. He, quite rightly in this role, is full of the medieval and Elizabethan awareness of death, which is so prevalent in all of Synge's work, and he becomes ultimately a kind of memento mori in his own person, choosing to lead the way into the grave. Lavarcham's comment about him in the final act again echoes *Hamlet* and clearly indicates the role in which Synge conceived him: "He went spying on Naisi, and now the worms is spying on his own inside."

Owen's reminders of imminent decay add to an uneasiness Deirdre has long felt, and Fergus's argument that she will not be young always strikes home. To all this, Synge adds the more dramatic scene in which Deirdre overhears Naisi admit to Fergus that he has begun to dread the moment when he may begin to weary of Deirdre and to show his weariness of her. Naisi's decision, despite his dread, is to stay in the more friendly woods rather than return to Emain Macha, and it is at Deirdre's insistence that they decide to return to what they know (through Owen, at least) will be certain death. All that has happened—and, in the act as it stands, there is God's plenty—has confirmed Deirdre in her dread of the loss of love through old age, the terrible, gradual attrition of love and of physical beauty and mastery that can be conquered only through the choice of a clean and early death. She knows, more clearly than ever, that "There's no place to stay always," and that "There's no safe place, Naisi, on the ridge of the world." Because this is the way the world is, she determines that it is "a better thing to be following on to a near death, than to be bending the head down, and dragging with the feet, and seeing one day a blight showing upon love."

In spite of the apparent idyl of the life in Alban, Deirdre has seen "in the quiet woods" the digging of their grave, with the clay thrown out "on leaves are bright and withered." The season is winter, and the image of the leaves bright and withered suggests frostbitten leaves, withered in their brightness, before the season for their natural decay and fall. The language of this passage and its specific reference to Deirdre's fears of loss are clear in her answer to Naisi's last plea to "Come away into the safety of the woods." She replies: "There are as many ways to wither love as there are stars in a night of Samhain. . . . It's for that we're setting out for Emain Macha when the tide turns on the sand." The image of the tide turning is as constant in this section as that of the storm in the first act. The tide of their lives is at its crest; and the return journey, to be made on the turning tide, represents Deirdre's acceptance of the natural cycle of life and necessity.

According to Yeats in "The Tragic Theatre," the third act of *Deirdre* is the only act that had satisfied Synge,[12] and the Deirdre of this last act is not so wearily ready for death as the woman of the second act. She hopes yet for peace between Conchubor and Naisi, and she has almost achieved it when Naisi's brothers cry out that they are under attack by Conchubor's men. Events have moved too swiftly even for Conchubor, and the man who has believed himself a maker of his own world by effort of his will is trapped by his own command into pursuit of an action that brings defeat or death to all of them.

Most of the last act takes place by the edge of the open grave prepared for the lovers, and the grave, like the dead Michael in *Riders to the Sea,* is an insistent presence on the stage. It is the little room Conchubor has readied to receive the sons of Usna that obtrudes into the land of the living; and ironically, there is nothing clean or quick about the first death to take place by its side—the death of kindness between Deirdre and Naisi. This moment is the most effective of Synge's unexpected reversals of the traditional material; it is the moment in which the unyielding realities of life betray the heroic actors of the tale, and Deirdre learns that, even more than she had guessed, death is "a poor, untidy thing, though it's a queen that dies." W. B. Yeats, with unerring instinct, cites the lines of the reversal as one of the moments of noblest tragedy in the play. Yeats tells us, in "The Tragic Theatre," "Deirdre and her lover . . . returned to Ireland . . . because death was better than broken love, and at the side of the open grave that had been dug for one and would serve for both, quarrelled, losing all they had given their life to keep."[13]

The quarrel between the lovers brings hard and bitter words, a pettiness that contrasts ironically their foolish desire to hurt each other with the seriousness of the situation and the traditional role that is being enacted. Deirdre's lament, "In a little while we've lived too long, Naisi, and isn't it a poor thing we should miss the safety of the grave, and we trampling its edge?" is one of the finest speeches of this or any play. Naisi's death and Deirdre's death, Fergus's return and burning of Emain Macha, and Conchubor's final knowledge of his loss inevitably seem a decline from this high moment of tragedy; but the desolation of humanity's lot is the insistent theme of the conclusion of the play. In spite of their quarrel, Deirdre refuses life without Naisi and chooses to be like him, young forever in the grave: "It is not a small thing to be rid of grey hairs and the loosening of the teeth. It was the choice of lives we had in the clear woods, and in the grave we're safe, surely."

The play ends in darkness; the burning fires of Emain Macha fade, and the grave, which, Deirdre reminds Conchubor, was "opened on a dark night," the night of the storm seven years ago, has triumphed. Fergus's epitaph, "four clear lights are quenched in Ireland," stresses the triumph of darkness over the desires and plans of man. And, when he throws his helpless sword into the grave, he acknowledges by symbolic action what Synge has demonstrated with the creation of his play: human beings, for all their heroic notions, for all their ideas and schemes, even for all their great passions, are doomed to defeat at the hands of life—"captives of destiny to be torn with beasts and gladiators—who appear only to destroy and be destroyed."

Conchubor remains, but he has seen the death of his desire and his subsequent defeat. He speaks with the voice of an old man; the proud and willful king must ask for direction and shelter. He is left with the desolation that his will has bought, a loss precisely expressed in the ruin of those halls and riches prepared to create a fortress against life and its ravages. Conchubor's words, "What we all need is a place is safe and splendid," contrasts ironically to Deirdre's prophecy when she sees the flames of Emain: "because of me there will be weasels and wild cats crying on a lonely wall where there were queens and armies and red gold. If nature mourned for man, Lavarcham says beside the grave, "it's a dark sky and a hard and naked earth we'd have this night in Emain." But nature does not mourn for humanity; it only covers over the spot where a king has tried to force his will, to insist on the possibility of his significant being. Where Conchubor's halls stood, "nettles will be growing and beyond thistles and docks." The deer and the goats will walk where the dreams of man have been, "and sheep waking and coughing when there is a great wind from the north." The clash of kings and the grand passions of tradition have served in Synge's hands to remind us that all lovers, love itself being mortal, quarrel this side of the grave, that topless towers are doomed to the thistles and the dock, and that swords have been doomed to rust since the beginning of time.

Chapter Nine

No Language but His Own

Poems

Synge will be remembered for the plays and *The Aran Islands,* but in addition to the prose work he left a small but important body of poems and translations. Although the translations have, generally, a secondary interest, Synge's poetic work, little known in his day or now, is of significance in its own right. Students of the plays may also find in the verse an additional statement of those attitudes that are explored in Synge's dramatic canon. Much of the poetry, however, is intensely personal in the way that dramatic statement, by its very definition, can never be; and Synge's failures and successes in the poetry help to explain the nature of his total achievement. As Yeats remarked, "In the arts," Synge knew "no language but his own," and an understanding of the ways in which Synge discovered and projected that language is extended and illuminated by an examination of his poems. It is in the poetry, according to John Masefield, that one finds the Synge that Masefield knew and talked to on Synge's infrequent visits to London: "The poems are the man speaking. They are so like him that to read them is to hear him."[1]

The man Masefield knew is hard to find in the early verse, however, for Synge's first poems have no voice distinguishable from that of his favorite poet, Wordsworth. The subject of these poems is nature, which in itself does not separate them from the body of Synge's poetry; but the controlling attitude, the vision of the artist who sees the world of the poem is not the same as that of the later work. Synge's first published verse, "Glencullen," appeared in the college publication, *Kottabos,* for Hilary Term, 1893, and the language and sentiment of this poem are much like those of an unpublished work of the same period, which is called, predictably enough, "A Mountain Creed."[2] In both poems nature is exalted for its own sake, and the sentiments of exaltation are borrowed from literature of the past, denying vitality to a subject most filled with a sense of life in the plays.

The "message" of "A Mountain Creed" is predictable from its opening lines:

> A mountain flower once I spied,
> A lonely height its dwelling,
> Where winds around it wailed and sighed
> Sad stories sadly telling.

The flower, despite its loneliness and the promise of sad stories sadly told, delights in fulfilling its proper role in the universe, which consists of being a jewel "'mid God's treasure." The language of the poem is as sentimental as its theme and resolution, and the treatment of the material, the soft reply of the flower to its unoriginal questioner, sounds nothing at all like the Synge we know through his later poetic or dramatic work. None of the poems before 1898 or 1899 have much that even suggests the later voice of the poet, but the poems after these dates reveal the slow growth of the kind of tensions so common in Synge's plays, tensions that the prose dramatic mode naturally seemed to call forth from the earliest plays.

During the last year of his life, having become a well-known, if not popular, dramatist, Synge diffidently undertook the preparation of his poems and translations for publication by the Cuala Press, choosing and revising the work of earlier years and writing several new pieces, although he did not live long enough to see his volume on the shelves of Dublin bookshops. During this period of surveying his poetic production, Synge rejected many of the early poems, regarding them as "boyish" verses, not fit for publication. The reasons for his rejections and his good judgment become clear when one reads the texts of these poems in volume 1 of the Oxford University Press edition of Synge's *Collected Works*.

Although an early experiment in the use of dialect may be found in a balladlike conversation between an acceptable member of society and a ragged pauper, most of these poems reveal the fact that Synge was no more able to write without the benefit of a controlling mask or distancing irony than he had been able in his youth to express himself publicly and directly as a performing musician. Even the poems in the *Vita Vecchia* sequence, written as the result of Synge's unsuccessful love affair with Cherrie Matheson, show little promise in spite of the care they received; for they never succeed in becoming anything more than

the outpourings—undistinguished and undistinguishable—of a young
man in the depths of his romantic agony.

The early poems, like the later, are full of the presence of death, and
Synge's development in the treatment of this most traditional poetic
subject may illustrate the essential difference between the earlier and
the later poems. One of these poems, "Epitaph," dated 189? by Robin
Skelton in the Oxford edition, was included by Synge in the Cuala
Press edition of 1909; but "Epitaph" is undoubtedly one of those
poems that, Synge warns in his introductory note, was written before
the ideas about the nature of poetry expressed in the preface had been
formulated. In "Epitaph" everything is traditional in treatment, romantic in attitude, and competent but unengaging:

> A silent sinner, nights and days,
> No human heart to him drew nigh,
> Alone he wound his wonted ways,
> Alone and little loved did die.
>
> And autumn Death for him did choose,
> A season dank with mists and rain,
> And took him, while the evening dews
> Were settling o'er the fields again.

The vagueness of the silent sinner is complete; he is silent, perhaps
because he is a solitary, a condition which may or may not be an out-
growth of his unspecified "sin"; on the other hand, one suspects his
silence may be better explained on alliterative grounds. At any rate,
there is nothing in this poem that is inevitable about the sinner, his
sin, his silence, his solitary condition, or the season of his death. Everything about the poem is gratuitous, including the syntax and the "poetic" words (*nigh, wonted, o'er*) as well as the personification of Death,
which is achieved by capitalization.

Among the poems published in the Cuala edition are several other
poems dealing with what is essentially the same theme: the ephemeral
nature of man's life, the presence and triumph of death, and man's
inability to mitigate the absolute victory of death. But these are poems
in which Synge has begun to find that voice that is "his own," poems
that *are* distinguishable from the work of other poets in the popular
nineteenth-century mode. For Synge was to discover that in verse as in

drama, energy comes from reality, strength from contact with things as they are. He was also to learn that the most individualized, the most personal voice is heard when it speaks out of some controlling attitude, which gives to verse tension and complexity. This tension came, for Synge, from an understanding that the poem is a momentary world, just as a stage is, and that the speaker (in Synge's case, usually the poet) defines himself against this world and by so doing creates the poem. Synge came, in other words, in his later and best poems to accept the need for the persona—the mask with its individual and definable stance—that provides the poem with the distance and control achieved in drama through character and scene, and the presence of the stage itself.

"To the Oaks of Glencree" might be called transitional in the course of this development. It too takes death as its subject and is included in the Cuala edition. It is quoted here in its entirety:

> My arms are round you, and I lean
> Against you, while the lark
> Sings over us, and golden lights and green
> Shadows are on your bark.
>
> There'll come a season when you'll stretch
> Black boards to cover me:
> Then in Mount Jerome I will lie, poor wretch,
> With worms eternally.

The first stanza establishes the romantic mood of the poet, speaking to the living oaks of Glencree as if to a lover, but it is the second stanza in juxtaposition to the first that does the work in this poem by presenting a statement that brutally betrays and comments upon the traditional attitudinizing of the first four lines. The oaks that living provide the poet a heightened consciousness of life will, in another season, stretch to cover him—not in the lover's embrace the words suggest, but, as the reader perceives with a shock, in a lifeless and unnatural form. The natural golden lights, green shadows on the bark of the oak, will be traded for black coffin boards (*black* in the literal color sense and colloquially, *evil*) to serve for the poet's burial in the Mount Jerome cemetery (where the Synge family plot was located); notice Synge's use of the concrete detail instead of the abstract generality of the earlier poems.

The self-pitying term "poor wretch" is partially qualified by the context of the poem, by the reality that intrudes in the form of death, both for the poet as conventional lover ("My arms are round you. . . .") and as the object of love. Both will lie with the worms "eternally," but the poet's "I will lie," the words of the self-concerned human being, become an index to the limits of human sympathy and create a context in which the posture of the first stanza is to be read.

In this poem Synge is dramatizing an implicit comment on poetic attitudes, the stuff of poetry. This poem seems almost to give substance to his specific statement about poetry in the preface to the poems and translations:

I have often thought that at the side of the poetic diction, which everyone condemns, modern verse contains a great deal of poetic material, using poetic in the same special sense. The poetry of exaltation will be always the highest, but when men lose their poetic feeling for ordinary life, and cannot write poetry of ordinary things, their exalted poetry is likely to lose its strength of exaltation, in the way men cease to build beautiful churches when they have lost happiness in building shops. . . .

In these days poetry is usually a flower of evil or good [Baudelaire or Tennyson?], but it is the timber of poetry that wears most surely, and there is no timber that has not strong roots among the clay and worms. Even if we grant that exalted poetry can be kept successful by itself, the strong things of life are needed in poetry also, to show what is exalted, or tender, is not made by feeble blood. It may almost be said that before verse can be human again it must learn to be brutal.

A return of poetry to the touchstone of the human condition is necessary as a corrective to the poetry of Coleridge and Shelley, which "went into verse that was not always human."

The human and the brutal are brought together in a late (1908) poem that found its way into the Cuala edition, a volume Synge was preparing as he worked on his last play, *Deirdre of the Sorrows,* itself full of the tragedy of death and decay. This poem, "A Question," is based on an incident that Yeats records in *The Death of Synge,* in which he states that Molly Allgood was asked by Synge if she would go to his funeral. Her reply, "No, for I could not bear to see you dead and the others living," sets the emotional tone for the last stanza of the poem in which the particularization, the sense of real speech between real people, has brought Synge a long way from the vagueness of situation and emotion of his first "Epitaph."

> I asked if I got sick and died, would you
> With my black funeral go walking too
> If you'd stand close to hear them talk or pray
> While I'm let down in that steep bank of clay.
> And, No, you said, for if you saw a crew
> Of living idiots, pressing round that new
> Oak coffin—they alive, I dead beneath
> That board—you'd rave and rend them with your teeth.

Having faced the problem of the poet's relationship to conventional material and attitudes, Synge quite naturally carried his discoveries into the area of traditional *Irish* material. The result was the creation of several of his best poems, in which he rejects the traditional in favor of immediate reality and infuses, in the course of examining the mythical material, an energy into the reality he prefers. "The Passing of the Shee," a response to one of A. E.'s pictures, is a good example of Synge's poetry of this kind, proceeding typically by means of a rather brutal contrast between the ideal and the real, the imagined world and the actual, with life and energy providing the more than adequate weight necessary to tip the scales in favor of Red Dan Sally's ditch.

> Adieu, sweet Angus, Maeve and Fand,
> Ye plumed yet skinny Shee,
> That poets played with hand in hand
> To learn their ecstasy.
> We'll search in Red Dan Sally's ditch,
> And drink in Tubber fair,
> Or poach with Red Dan Philly's bitch
> The badger and the hare.

The poetic diction appropriate to the material of the first stanza and a part of the poet's equipment for dealing with the world of the Shee, the supernatural creatures of Irish legend, is abandoned by Synge in the second stanza of the poem; in it the pursuit of the vital takes the poet into the ditch, the fair, the field. It is not the second stanza alone that is brutal, however, for the treatment of the material of the first is contemptuous in tone. The Shee *are* skinny in the sense that they are insubstantial; yet *skinny* is not a neutral word. Also, Synge, by his insistence upon the phonetic spelling *Shee* (instead of the proper and more pretentious spelling *Sidhe*) makes a comment on the whole of the ancient Irish tradition in the modern world. *Sidhe,* the Gaelic word for *wind* as well as for the supernatural beings who are associated with the winds, suggests the basis for the popular portrayal of these creatures as airy, light, and insubstantial—a portrayal that justifies the description, skinny, when viewed from the ditch.

As an Irish poet, Synge faced the same problem as Yeats and others, for poetry of a certain kind, in the years at the turn of the century, seemed almost a national duty. Synge passed through the same evolutionary process as Yeats in respect to nationalism, feeling that the Irish ballad poetry of *The Spirit of the Nation* school was excellent, and then, as his tastes matured, repenting bitterly this "most serious literary error."[3] Unlike Yeats, however, Synge never sought to re-create in the present an idealized Irish past. His youthful interest in Ireland's history was from the first an antiquarian one, and there was never a time in which he envisioned the return of a heroic Ireland as had Yeats and Maud Gonne. Synge's abiding dislike of Tennyson, even in these formative years, was undoubtedly a part of an instinctive avoidance of idealization and heroic abstraction.

"Queens," one of Synge's few long poems and one of his best, has for its subject the royal queens of legend and history. In this poem the poet fulfills his traditional function of naming, of invoking the rich connotations associated with names of famous and beautiful women of the past; but Synge, by his repeated naming of these queens in the context of reality as it must have been even in the legendary past, brings into play an echo of the special Renaissance context for the word *queen,* which is invoked simultaneously with the mythic and traditional contexts of the names of past queens. These are "rare and royal names" the poet calls forth; yet they are, because of their human aspects, also

> Queens whose finger once did stir men,
> Queens were eaten of fleas and vermin,
> Queens men drew like Monna Lisa,
> Or slew with drugs in Rome and Pisa,
> . . . .
> And Titian's lady with amber belly,
> Queens acquainted in learned sin.

The tone mocks the pretensions time has given to the names of these dead ladies.

"Queens" owes a great deal to Villon's ballad from which Synge borrowed "Bert, the big-foot, sung by Villon," a ballad best known in English literature through Dante Rossetti's translation, "The Ballad of Dead Ladies." Instead of the "snows of yesteryear" formula, however, Synge ties his conclusion to the present, so that his poem becomes a commentary on the condition of live lovers and poets as well as on dead queens.

The word *rotten* becomes crucial to the ironic statement the poem makes in its last four lines:

> Yet these are rotten—I ask their pardon—
> And we've the sun on rock and garden,
> These are rotten, so you're the Queen
> Of all are living, or have been.

The queens traditionally celebrated by poets are rotten because they are dead and rotten in the grave; they are also rotten, however, because corruption is an inevitable part of the human condition. The poet of the poem seems at first to insist that whatever has life, real physical existence—"the sun on rock and garden"—is superior thereby to all that is dead, no matter how rare and royal in the past. The superiority of the poet's lady love to queens of the past is clear enough on such a basis, but the concluding line becomes an ironic statement about the poet as lover, and it qualifies the elevation of his lady love over all the "rotten" queens of the past, for it partakes—in spite of all the poet has demonstrated that he knows in his roll call of dead queens—of the traditional, poetic inflation that has given legendary proportions to the queens of the past.

Having rejected the traditional in general and the legendary Irish material in particular, Synge understandably looked close at hand for his poetic subjects, and found them either in his immediate personal experience (in such poems as "Dread," "I've Thirty Months," "In Kerry") or in the observed Irish scene that had provided him the materials for his prose. "On an Island" is typical of these peasant poems, presenting a scene that Synge had described in *The Aran Islands.* Synge's poetry, which results from his conscious growth as an artist, like his best drama begins in a feeling for the ordinary. The world of

"On an Island" is created out of the real and the explicit, out of an experienced reality that provides accurate and precise details that Synge embodies in an appropriately non-"poetic" language. He offers in this poem an alternative to the world of the "plumed yet skinny Shee," which is pallid and lifeless beside the world of an island woman who has, among her daily tasks, "plucked a curlew, drawn a hen, / Washed the sheets of seven men" before an evening of dancing to "jigs and reels" with "Nailed boots chasing girls' naked heels."

Several of Synge's poems using local material are cast in ballad form. One of these, "The 'Mergency Man," tells the story of a professional evictor who meets his end by drowning on a dark night when he had thought to catch the unsuspecting tenants with "a latch on the door." This poem has something of the ballad's objectivity, but it is not particularly distinguished in any other way, although the subject of land evictions was one that had moved Synge to a lengthy description in *The Aran Islands* and one about which he felt a personal responsibility, for his brother Edward had been involved in the eviction of tenants during Synge's boyhood with—according to Greene and Stephens's biography—a "brutal efficiency" that horrified the youngest Synge.[4]

The actual occurrence that gave Synge the material for his poem came to him from a story he had heard from a man in West Kerry. The story, one in which the teller takes evident delight, provides appropriate material for re-creation as a ballad. The account of the death of the 'mergency man, as Synge repeats it in the essay "In West Kerry," is full of details that make their way into the poem.

Twenty years ago they sent down a 'mergency man to lodge above by the lake and serve processes on the people, but the people were off before him and lay abroad in the heather. Then, in the course of a piece, a night came, with great rain out of the heavens, and my man said: "I'll get them this night in their own beds, surely," Then he let call the peelers—they had peelers waiting to mind him—and down they come to the big stepping-stones they have above for crossing the first river coming out of the lakes. My man going in front to cross over, and the water was high up covering the stones. Then he gave two leps or three, and the peelers heard him give a great shriek down in the flood. They went home after—what could they do?—and the 'mergency man was found in the sea stuck in a net.

In this same section of "In West Kerry" Synge reprints an art ballad he had heard at the Puck Fair, and he notes that it seemed "pitifully remote from any good spirit of ballad-making." Unlike "The 'Mergency Man" or "Danny," this ballad in honor of Puck is full of political digressions and editorial comments:

> Where is the tyrant dare oppose it?
> Our old customs we will hold up still,
> And I think we will have another—
> That is, Home Rule and Purchase Bill.

Synge's own ballads escape the temptation of editorial comment and present the narrative essence in the traditional manner. He makes no pause for description or comment, no intrusion of the speaker, in these essentially dramatic poems. His profound sense of the tradition of the native tale teller, which he demonstrates in *The Aran Islands* and *In Wicklow, West Kerry and Connemara*, turns him naturally toward an objective treatment of the 'mergency man and Danny.

"Danny" was one of several important poems not included in the Cuala Press edition of Synge's poems. It was published first by Maunsel in the year following Synge's death. "Danny" had been omitted from the Cuala Press edition because Elizabeth Yeats, the poet's sister and director of the press, found the ballad too strong in subject matter and language for readers' tastes. Completed the same year as *The Playboy of the Western World*, Synge's ballad (also based on an actual occurrence) tells the story of a young playboy named Danny, who is waylaid by nine-and-twenty lads who, in the interest of protecting "girls and widows," brutally murder Danny. In an excess of civic zeal these righteous citizens appropriate Danny's purse and timber pipe. Interestingly enough, W. B. Yeats did not pick up this poem when he selected some of Synge's work for an anthology he edited in 1936, but in his preface he praised Synge for the masculinity of his verse.

A short poem, "The Curse," had also been excluded from the Cuala edition by Elizabeth Yeats on the same grounds as "Danny," but her brother managed to reinstate "The Curse" by including the poem in his introduction. The full subtitle of this occasional poem reads, *"To a sister of an enemy of the author's who disapproved of 'The Playboy,'"* the subject of the poem being Molly Allgood's sister Mrs. Callender. "The Curse" is in the Irish tradition of the inflated (ergo, largely self-canceling) curse, the classic example being James Stephens's translation of David O'Bruadair's response to the barmaid who had refused him a drink: "May she marry a ghost and bear him a kitten, and may / The

High King of Glory permit her to get the mange." Synge's curse joins
the traditions of the occasional poem and the Irish curse:

> Lord, confound this surly sister,
> Blight her brow with blotch and blister,
> Cramp her larynx, lung, and liver,
> In her guts a galling give her.
> Let her live to earn her dinners
> In Mountjoy with seedy sinners.
> Lord, this judgment quickly bring,
> And I'm your servant, J. M. Synge.

The language of Synge's "Curse," its directness and strength, contrasts
sharply with his early work, and there is here a full measure of that
rough and brutal (if, on this occasion, good-humored) reality that most
effectively sets Synge's work apart from the general tendencies in romantic, Victorian, or Georgian poetry.

In his preface to the Cuala poems Yeats also records a comment of
Synge's that seemed to him important, "We must unite asceticism,
stoicism, ecstasy; two of these have often come together but not all
three. . . ." And Yeats concludes:

the strength that made him delight in setting the hard virtues by the soft,
the bitter by the sweet, salt by mercury, the stone by the elixir, gave him a
hunger for harsh facts, for ugly surprising things, for all that defies our hope.
In "The Passing of the Shee" he is repelled by the contemplation of a beauty
too far from life to appease his mood; and in his own work, benign images
ever present to his soul must have beside them malignant reality, and the
greater the brightness the greater must the darkness be.

Yeats felt that Synge had succeeded in uniting "asceticism, stoicism,
ecstasy," and his belief in Synge's achievement persisted, so that,
within a few years of his own death, Yeats acted upon his conviction
by giving to Synge's verse a disproportionately large representation in
the *Oxford Book of Modern Verse*. The early books of Synge's poems had
received little notice, and it must have been something of a shock for
readers of Yeats's edition of the *Oxford Book of Modern Verse* in 1936 to
discover Synge, a man whose reputation established him as playwright
and not as a poet, represented by eight poems and four translations. It
is hard to understand the emphasis and proportion given to Synge in
Yeats's edition; for the poems that were certainly startling in the first

decade of the twentieth century lacked even this value by the mid-1930s. Yeats's insistent inclusion of Synge's work is perhaps to be explained by reference to his claim in the introduction that "John Synge brought back masculinity to Irish verse with his harsh disillusionment." But not even Yeats's introductory comment can account for the presence of Synge's early Wordsworthian poem, "Prelude," in the *Oxford Book of Modern Verse.*

There is little doubt that Synge's work, both poetic and dramatic, had its share of influence on Yeats's own work; but it is easy to overstate the case, as the tendency of recent critics has shown.[5] A most sensible estimate of this influence is to be found in T. R. Henn's measured chapter, "Yeats and Synge," in *The Lonely Tower* (1950). Although Synge had chosen the poems for the Cuala edition, to Yeats fell the task of gathering Synge's poems for posthumous publication by Maunsel in 1910, and among those he added were "The 'Mergency Man," "I've Thirty Months," and "In Kerry"—poems that seemed to him to bear out the promise of Synge's particular poetic genius. This task of working with Synge's papers and poems undoubtedly left its mark on Yeats's own work, but there can be no question that Yeats was already moving in the direction of a more "masculine" verse when he discovered Synge's poetic achievement. The case is somewhat analogous to the influence of the Noh drama on Yeats's Dance Plays: Yeats had been moving in the direction of a formalized, symbolic, aristocratic theater before he was exposed to the Japanese traditional form through contact with Ezra Pound, demonstrating simply that influence is in direct proportion to preparation and receptivity. In short, Synge offered to Yeats an example of what the established poet had already seen as a possibility, and he left the better poet to bring this possibility to realization.

Plays in Verse

Although this study of Synge's work is concerned only with his established, published canon, the printing of the material of several fragmentary verse plays in the Greene and Stephens biography and in the first volume of the Oxford edition of the *Collected Works* lends support to the idea that Synge was capable of writing in a "neutral" or non-Syngean manner, a phenomenon that also occurs in his literary essays and reviews.

These fragments are of limited interest except by way of demonstrating, like the early Wordsworthian poems, how important to Synge's creation was the discovery of a native voice. Although these verse plays have Irish settings and Irish place names, and even some of Synge's principal subjects, Synge has accepted the stereotype of the nineteenth-century verse play for his model, and it is only briefly that his own voice breaks through the traditional mold.

All of these verse plays were begun in 1902, the same year that Synge worked on *Riders to the Sea, The Shadow of the Glen,* and had begun *The Tinker's Wedding.* Surveying the products of this year of remarkable creativity, we can have no doubt that Synge's decision to abandon the verse plays and to accept the rhythmic prose idiom as his dramatic vehicle was a wise one   one that made possible his unique contribution to the literature of the stage. The fragmentary verse plays that are printed in the Oxford volume are conventional and traditional in language, attitude, and situation. The predominant line Synge uses is in the traditional iambic of English verse, a foot that defeats the Anglo-Irish rhythms that Synge is able to create for his prose dramas. The iambic pentameter line of the conventional blank verse that tradition decreed for verse drama in English is confining enough, but Synge chose to cast two of his verse plays into rhymed couplets, and this use of the heroic couplet most often means the addition of a forced rhyme to an already lifeless line.

The longest of the verse fragments, *The Vernal Play,* is, as its name suggests, a play cast in the pastoral mode, and its subjects are familiar to the readers of *Deirdre*—the inevitable death and decay attendant upon life and love. In this play, however, one finds the gratuitous juxtaposition of these important aspects of existence: life and death, youth and age, love and loss. The formal lament, or the keen that the young make for the death of the old man in the stormy night, illustrates the presence of this juxtaposition, but the treatment here is that of the traditional lament of the romantic poet, with the result that this material does not become operative in dramatic terms, as does, say, Deirdre's lament over the grave of Naisi.

> Etain.   All young girls must yield to rage.
>   All firm youth must end in age.
> Boinn.   I call the lambs that browse with fright,
>   To mourn the man who died tonight.
> Niave.   Every eye must fade and blear,
>   Every bone bleach bare and clear.
> Boinn.   All must rise from earth and clay.
>   All must end in green decay. . . .[6]

The apparent oxymoron of "green decay" is effective, even familiar, perhaps, to readers of Dylan Thomas's poetry; but most of the keen (even though it does break momentarily with the persistent, dulling pentameter line) is forced and unconvincing. Synge's rendering of *Et in Arcadia ego* is simply not very original.

The other fragment in heroic couplets—though extremely brief, and belonging to a play Synge probably never completed (unlike the other two fragments, which were parts of finished works that were subsequently destroyed)[7]—is of more interest to the student of Synge's development as a playwright than is the pastoral play. In the brief lines of *The Lady O'Conor* Synge attempted to create dramatic material in verse out of one of the stories he had heard from Pat Dirane in the Aran Islands, which Synge recounted in its entirety in *The Aran Islands* because it contained many elements of European folk literature.

The scenario of the projected verse play, printed in Appendix C of the Oxford edition, shows that Synge intended to use all of Pat Dirane's long and involved story in a dramatic creation of four acts—at best a complicated undertaking. The dialogue between the Lady O'Conor, O'Conor, and the captain is of real interest, for Synge (perhaps under the influence of Pat Dirane's telling of the old motifs) tries to work peasant dialect to fit the pattern of his iambic pentameter lines. The results are still largely (and necessarily) artificial, but the effect moves Synge closer to the language of the prose plays than had the less engaging dialogue of *The Vernal Play*.

The third fragment, *Luasnad, Capa and Laine,* belonging to this period is based on a legend about Ireland's first inhabitants. The legend is repeated in Geoffrey Keating's *The History of Ireland.* According to Keating, there is no certainty about the first inhabitants of Ireland, but they may have been "three fishermen who were driven by a storm of wind from Spain unwillingly; and as the island pleased them that they returned for their wives to Spain; and having come back to Ireland again, the deluge was showered upon them at Tuaigh Innbhir, so that they were drowned. Capa, Laighne and Luasad, their names."[8] Synge's intention, worked out in his notebook, was to show the three men and their wives sitting on a rock and watching the deluge overwhelm the world. Finally only Luasnad and Laine's wife are left of them all, and Luasnad makes love to the woman to assert their will to life in the face of the death that at last overtakes them.

This fragment differs from the others by being in blank verse, but even so it is a verse indistinguishable from anybody's blank verse in nineteenth-century England, and the subject—human defeat by the universe—although one Synge could treat eloquently in prose, is strangely deadened by his formal poetics.

The problem of poetic drama was one that preoccupied Synge throughout his life, and one that he identified with the problems of historical drama, tradition having made historical events the fit and proper subject matter for verse drama. In his *Deirdre* Synge rejected the inevitable union of historical subject matter and verse treatment, and this rejection was the result of long and careful thought about the nature of beauty and poetry in drama. His conclusion that "for the present the only possible beauty in drama is peasant drama. For the future we must await the making of life beautiful again before we can have beautiful drama,"[9] must have come long before March 1907, when he recorded it in his notebook. He had rejected his experiments in verse and sought the creation of a drama in which he fashioned a prose dialogue based on Anglo-Irish speech rhythms that served the purposes both of poetry and of reality. His solution in rhythmic prose answered the objection he raised in his notebook at the same time: "The real world is mostly unpoetical; fiction even in poetry is not totally sincere, hence the failure of modern poetry."[10]

The problem of verse drama in particular and of poetic drama generally is one that has not yet been adequately solved for modern writers. It is a problem to which T. S. Eliot devoted a great deal of concern and energy, and his conclusions about Synge's solution are of interest, for they acknowledge the success of Synge's achievement while pointing out the limitations of Synge's answer to the general problem of drama in verse:

At this point I might say a word about those plays which we call *poetic,* though they are written in prose. The plays of John Millington Synge form rather a special case, because they are based upon the idiom of a rural people whose speech is naturally poetic, both in imagery and in rhythm. . . . The language of Synge is not available except for plays set among that same people. . . . Synge wrote plays about characters whose originals in life talked poetically, so he could make them talk poetry and remain real people.[11]

Synge's language, which most critics agree was a large part of his contribution to the development of the Irish theater, grew out of his desire to recapture the vitality of a living speech suitable for communicating the concerns of real men. His interest in the success of the oral tradition in Ireland is the subject of an essay he worked on in his notebooks, and his meditations on this subject brought him to see a double life for poetry, "in the voice of the poet and in the voice of the reader, who is, or should be a kind of performer." Synge felt that the sound of the poet's voice had been lost from poetry, causing it to become lifeless and "one-dimensional."[12] The attempt to restore the speaker's voice, to find again the idiom of a living people, led Synge to work with his translations of other authors into peasant dialect, an exercise directly related to and growing out of his major interests.

Translations

Synge's translations turn the language of Villon, Leopardi, von der Vogelweide, Petrarch, and Colin Muset into an Anglo-Irish prose dialect that gives his work a distinctive and vital quality seldom shared by other translators. Synge, in the free rendering of his sources, succeeds in creating from the original a new product, perhaps, but certainly one full of a strength and immediacy usually lost in the process of translation.

A comparison of several stanzas of Dante Gabriel Rossetti's translation of Villon, "His Mother's Service to Our Lady," with a comparable part of Synge's translation of the same material, "Prayer of the Old Woman, Villon's Mother," indicates the unique quality of Synge's achievement, something made possible by the adoption of the Anglo-Irish voice and by abandonment of that traditional, neutral stance so evident in the plays in verse. Compare the following from Rossetti:

> A pitiful poor woman, shrunk and old,
>   I am, and nothing learn'd in letter-lore.
> Within my parish-cloister I behold
>   A painted Heaven where harps and lutes adore.
>   And eke an Hell whose damned folk seethe full sore:
> One bringeth fear, the other joy to me.
> That joy, great Goddess, make thou mine to be,—
>   Thou of whom all must ask it even as I;
> And that which faith desires, that let it see.
>   For in this faith I choose to live and die.
>
> O excellent Virgin Princess! thou didst bear
> King Jesus, the most excellent comforter,
> Who even of this our weakness craved a share,
>   And for our sake stooped to us from on high,

Offering to death His young life sweet and fair.
Such as He is, Our Lord, I Him declare,
And in this faith I choose to live and die.

with this from Synge:

I'm a poor aged woman, was never at school, and is no scholar with letters, but I've seen pictures in the chapel with Paradise on one side, and harps and pipes in it, and the place on the other side, where sinners do be boiled in torment; the one gave me great joy, the other a great fright and scaring, let me have the good place, Mother of God, and it's in your faith I'll live always.

It's yourself that bore Jesus, that has no end or death, and He the Lord Almighty, that took our weakness and gave Himself to sorrows, a young and gentle man. It's Himself is our Lord surely, and it's in that faith I'll live always.

Synge's interest in translations had been excited by his friendship with the American Poet, Agnes Tobin, who had done her own translations of Petrarch's sonnets. There is general agreement that Synge's own translations were begun late in his life for the purpose of practice in dialect or for self-discipline in writing Anglo-Irish. Skelton suggests that these exercises were directly connected with Synge's concern for finding a style that could carry the heroic material of his *Deirdre of the Sorrows* and yet retain the vitality, strength, and simplicity he associated with the peasant idiom, which had its roots in the experienced and actual.[13]

The Anglo-Irish idiom with which Synge was working in his plays and translations has been described in some detail by the German philologist, A. G. van Hamel in his article, "On Anglo-Irish Syntax." Van Hamel finds two principal causes that account for the existence of Anglo-Irish as a distinctive mode of expression:

In the seventeenth century English was introduced [into Ireland] by a large number of English settlers, but after that time no immigration of importance took place. Therefore English was not exposed to the same influences in Ireland as in England and, being more secluded in the former country than in the latter, it preserved many features that remind us of the seventeenth century. On the other hand, English did not spread among the common people in Ireland until recently, and even now it still has to force back the old Celtic speech. The Irish peasants . . . did not only experience great difficulties in trying to pronounce sounds very different from their own, but also in adopting

English idioms and constructions. Gaelic is a very idiomatic language, and it is but natural that the Irish should have begun speaking English by translating Gaelic phrases into English words.[14]

Part of the war that raged over Synge's presentation of the Irish scene inevitably touched on the language that he chose to use. Accusations of a failure to render faithfully his Irish sources had resulted in Synge's defensive remarks about his characters' language in the preface to *The Playboy of the Western World*. The objections to Synge's language had persisted long and loudly enough to call forth an explanation from L. A. G. Strong in his essay on Synge: "The language of Synge's plays is *not* the language of the peasants, insomuch that no peasant talks consistently as Synge's characters talk: it *is* the language of the peasants, in that it contains no word or phrase a peasant did not actually use."[15] Synge's language in his plays and translations is, then, a heightened use of an authentic speech and its rhythms.

Synge's Anglo-Irish style came largely from his own observation, a process of listening to a speech in which his own knowledge of Gaelic and its constructions stood him in good stead. He also had literary antecedents in Ireland, however, for the tongue he was to use. These were, principally, in his immediate background—Douglas Hyde, Lady Gregory, and, to a lesser degree, W. B. Yeats. All three are commended for their contributions to the language in Synge's 1902 review of Lady Gregory's *Cuchulain of Muirthemne* in the *Speaker* for 7 June. Lady Gregory's idiom in her book was, Synge felt, "a simple and powerful language that resembles a good deal the peasant dialect of the west of Ireland," and he later won Lady Gregory's gratitude by telling her that in her *Cuchulain* he had found the dialect for which he had been searching: "Your *Cuchulain* is part of my daily bread."

The essays and reviews Synge wrote for a number of periodicals gave him a chance to evaluate the language being used to give voice to the Irish cultural revival and to formulate his own ideas about the language that seemed right for expression of Irish subjects in English. Synge's conclusion was unequivocal: an Irish literature must have a distinctive voice, which seemed to him most clearly present in the Anglo-Irish speech of the peasants of the west of Ireland, where the Gaelic influence on English had been most retained. As Synge's remarks in his essay "The Irish Literary Movement" demonstrate, a literature in English, untouched by Gaelic, is too closely tied to England to be expressive of Irish culture. The problems that Synge defined in this essay were those

that he himself had faced, and the answers that he suggests for the
Irish writer had led him to the speech of the peasants of the "Western
world," the Anglo-Irish dialect, which, combined with his discoveries
of the relationship between the voice and the speaker, gave to Synge
that special "language of his own."

Chapter Ten
A Young Man's Ghost
Among Peers

When Yeats spoke to the Swedish Royal Academy during his visit in Stockholm to receive the Nobel Prize for literature in 1923, he chose to speak on the Irish dramatic movement. He said, "When your King gave me medal and diploma, two forms should have stood, one at either side of me, an old woman sinking into the infirmity of age, and a young man's ghost. I think when Lady Gregory and John Synge's name are spoken by future generations, my name, if remembered, will come up in their talk, and that if my name is spoken first their names will come in their turn."[1] Synge had become in Yeats's mind and in the memory of others a part of the essential trinity of the Abbey Theatre, in spite of the fact that it was Edward Martyn and not he who was present as the third member of the founding triumvirate. At the time Yeats, Lady Gregory, and Martyn were meeting to create their ideal of an Irish dramatic movement, Synge was merely an interested observer, who still considered Paris the center of his activities and criticism the end of his intellectual concern. Nor was Synge, like the others, actively concerned with the movement for Irish national independence; he was a gradualist in politics, who had resigned from the Irish League in Paris after a few months' membership because he found himself in conflict with the methods of the group.

Synge's eminence in the Irish theater and in Yeats's generous description before the Swedish Royal Academy resulted from the simple fact that he was, in the first decade of the century, the best playwright among the Irish writers, and they knew it. A "man of genius" is the phrase that recurs in contemporary descriptions of Synge to the extent that Yeats's publisher complained that the support and praise Synge received was detracting from Yeats's own reputation.[2] Synge gave the Abbey the sense of having genius in its midst (however difficult this was to prove), and the leaders of the theater movement gave to Synge a warmth of welcome that few young and untried artists have received.

Yeats had not yet entered his major period as a playwright when

Synge came to the Irish theater group with two completed plays and a third in process. Yeats had then seen his own *Land of Heart's Desire, The Countess Cathleen, The Pot of Broth, Cathleen ni Houlihan,* and *The Hour-Glass*—all relatively slight plays—staged before the first performance of *The Shadow of the Glen. Riders to the Sea* was presented on the stage in the same month as an early version of *The Shadowy Waters,* creating a contrast that cannot have been lost on Yeats, who continued working on his play for a number of years; he sought for it more strength and a clearer outline, until he arrived at a final version in which T. R. Henn finds the occasional influence of Synge.[3] It is not possible to know how much influence Synge actually had on Yeats, the infinitely greater artist; but it is very possible that Synge acted as a catalyst for Yeats as he moved from his early romantic style toward his later, more modern style. Synge's plays, like his poetry, suggested to Yeats what could be made of Irish material without the surrounding aura of traditional Irish romantic mists, how the world of *The Wanderings of Oisin* could be transformed in *The Death of Cuchulain.* "The Passing of the Shee" trades the world of the "plumed yet skinny Shee" for that of "Red Dan Philly's bitch / The badger and the hare," an exchange that Yeats makes in the course of his development (a producing career nearly five times as long as Synge's). Cathleen must yield to Crazy Jane, who, like Mary Byrne, thinking on Emer and Cuchulain and all that world, lies "stretched out in the dirt"—perhaps of Red Dan Sally's ditch?

It would be easy enough to overestimate Synge's specific influence on Yeats, but the best and safest gauge of Synge's relationship to Yeats's career is the fact that Yeats found in Synge a symbolic figure, a man who entered into his imaginative world as a very real and substantial presence for the extent of Yeats's life. Several critics, among them Herbert Howarth in *The Irish Writers,* take Yeats to task for his imperfect memory and exaggerated claims of influencing Synge to go to Aran or in the conception of *The Playboy of the Western World,* as well as for the use to which Yeats put the *Playboy* controversy. Yeats's subsequent treatment of Synge needs no apology, however; for, whatever inaccuracies it may contain, it is always generous and proceeds out of an emotional content the figure of Synge held for Yeats, which was itself far in excess of the response generated by the personal friendship of the two men. Yeats's harmless misrepresentations do not detract from Synge's achievement; instead, they signify Yeats's involvement with the meaning that the "young man's ghost" came to have for him. In the events of Synge's lifetime as a playwright Yeats found support for his own decision to turn his energies away from an attempt to create a people's theater for an unappreciative people.

Yeats returns to the figure of Synge in a number of his poems—particularly when he calls the roll of the creative leaders of the Irish renaissance—Hyde, Synge, Lady Gregory, Shawe-Taylor, and Hugh Lane. In "Ireland after the Revolution" Yeats specifically states: "Berkeley, Swift, Burke, Grattan, Parnell, Augusta Gregory, Synge, Kevin O'Higgins, are the true Irish people, and there is nothing too hard for such as these."[4]

Synge was for Yeats always the meditative man, the man apart from excitement, separated by character and will from the volatile center of the Irish movement. Yet Synge is, in "In Memory of Major Robert Gregory," a part of the essential Irish scene, a man who "dying chose the living world for text," and found that world in "a most desolate stony place," peopled by "a race / Passionate and simple like his heart." And in "The Municipal Gallery Revisited," Synge, Yeats, and Lady Gregory are separated from others in "modern times" for understanding that all that would grow strong must come from contact with the soil:

> We three alone in modern times had brought
> Everything down to that sole test again,
> Dream of the noble and the beggar-man.

John Synge, "that rooted man" who never gave himself to distraction, seemed always to Yeats to embody a passionate strength, a tie with the earth, that Yeats increasingly sought for his own work. Synge's emphasis on "joy" and "reality" became a part of Yeats's own tragic and poetic theory; and, while Yeats most surely would have found his artistic growth without Synge, he had in the tragic death of Synge an event that engaged him wholly, that gave imaginative substance to that which he had learned from the man living.

Synge found his way into Yeats's *Vision,* to take his place beside Rembrandt as Yeats's embodiment of "The Receptive Man in Phase Twenty-Three." Although Synge is used to represent a general type, Yeats's comments suggest the meaning of Synge's accomplishment for him; and they provide, incidentally, quite an accurate picture of the man who emerges from a reading of the plays. The wisdom of the man of this phase is that of "general humanity experienced as a form of involuntary emotion and involuntary delight in the 'minute particulars' of life. The man wipes his breath from the window-pane, and laughs in his delight at all the varied scene." The *Will* of this man, according to Yeats, is in revolt "from every intellectual summary, from all intellectual abstraction," and therefore his delight "is not mere delight, he would construct a whole, but that whole must seem all event, all picture." Yet, in spite of his insistence on the whole scene, this man cares "only for what is human, individual and moral. To others he may seem to care for the immoral and inhuman only, for he will be hostile, or indifferent to moral as to intellectual summaries . . . if he is Synge he takes a malicious pleasure in the contrast between his hero, whom he discovers through his instinct for comedy, and any hero in men's minds. Indeed, whether he be Synge or Rembrandt, he is ready to sacrifice every convention, perhaps all that men have agreed to reverence, for a startling theme."[5] The image Yeats draws of the man of the twenty-third phase is one that evokes all that was antithetical to Yeats's own nature and suggests Synge's particular value to Yeats, both personal and artistic; for Yeats strove throughout his life to take to himself and his art those qualities that seemed most alien to the nature of the Yeats who was Synge's contemporary.

Synge's personal relationships within what may roughly be defined as the Irish literary movement were few, and they largely grew out of his work. His lasting personal friendship with Stephen MacKenna and his briefer friendship with Jack Yeats seem to have been exceptions, for his relationships with his coworkers were generally cordial but dispassionate. Synge and Lady Gregory respected each other's abilities, but he was never taken under her generous wing in the way that Yeats was, although Synge readily acknowledged his debt to Lady Gregory's example in the use of peasant speech.[6] Although not in any deep way, Synge was rather more in Lady Gregory's debt than the other way around; but his plays (particularly *The Playboy,* which she hated but defended even in the face of threats to her personal safety) gave her an opportunity to fight for the right of artistic integrity in Ireland. She may have gotten a few hints for the imaginatively sustaining relationship between her old people in *The Workhouse Ward* from *The Well of the Saints,* but if so, the debt may have been repaid with Synge's knowledge of *The Spreading of the News* before he came to write *The Playboy of the Western World.* The constant contact and close relationship of the workers of the theater movement make it impossible to trace all the debts and influences of the principals. Suffice it to say that as a director of the Abbey Theatre company for a brief time and as a playwright over a period of seven years, Synge in actuality and in the eyes of his peers pulled his weight and gave as much, if not more, than he took.

The Influence

Herbert Howarth in *The Irish Writers* finds Synge's general influence on the Irish literary movement to have been considerable enough to have "determined its success and at the same time altered its direction. After his death it developed in his way rather than in the way that Yeats, who had recruited him to it, had previously supposed it should." Synge, as Howarth suggests and as Yeats knew, was invaluable because he stood against those who were full of enthusiasms at the cost of reality. "He would have no literary truck with Messiahs. The bent of his mind was against the good news of the evangelists."[7] And this opposition included the political evangelists who would bend all things toward national ends, no matter what distortions the bendings caused. Synge hauled the harshness of reality onto the misty idealized stage that had been set for Ireland's destiny. J. B. Yeats knew what he was doing and what Synge had done when, asking an angry mob for a hearing for *The Playboy of the Western World,* the elder Yeats referred to Ireland as "This Land of Saints," and when the applause began he added, "his beautiful mischievous head thrown back," "'Of plaster Saints,'"[8]

What Synge had done, no Irish playwright could undo. Those who followed Synge on the Abbey roster owed much to him for their direction. Padraic Colum and Sean O'Casey, to name only two, succeeded in making a dramatic world that insisted on Synge's kind of truth without, perhaps, the absolute and uncompromising quality of his vision.

At the end of his life Synge was thinking about the necessity for shifting his attention to the drama of the city, of moving his scene from the small village and the countryside into the streets and slums of the growing urban areas. He did not live to undertake this new area for dramatic expression, but one of his countrymen, James Joyce, did; and Joyce himself seems to have been aware of his debt to Synge.[9] Although *The Playboy of the Western World* is more obviously akin to his own achievement, Joyce (in spite of his typical ambivalence toward his Irish contemporaries) admired *Riders to the Sea* enough to complete an Italian translation of the play, thus adding to Synge's growing international reputation. Joyce had even undertaken preliminary negotiations for a performance of *Riders to the Sea* in Italy in 1909 before he discovered that Synge's heirs would refuse permission for the performance.[10]

Reputation at Home and Abroad

Although his name was anathema to many Irishmen, Synge's plays were given performances on the Continent during his lifetime, and his work generally found a receptive audience outside of Ireland. The English received Synge's plays with favor (a fact that confirmed certain Irish critics of the playwright in their views of the subversive nature of his work), and performances of *The Shadow of the Glen* were arranged with Synge by Pan Karel Musek for Prague audiences. *The Well of the Saints* was performed in Germany with small success, but in general the continental reception of Synge's work was more congenial than that it received in Ireland, where Owen Quinn, as late as 1950, could insist that Synge's work was "unlikely to have any bearing, except in a negative way," on the future of Irish literature.[11]

In spite of Quinn's pronouncement, a recognition of Synge's place in Irish literature has grown steadily, and the long delayed publication of many of his papers and of the official biography finally make possible an understanding of Synge's place in the Irish literary movement. The reaction to his work has always been an excessive one, either in damning or praising it; and the very persistence of excessive reaction may provide a final comment on his importance. Seldom in the history of literature has such a small body of work occasioned such a large-scale reaction. According to Yeats, Synge "was but the more hated because he gave his country what it needed, an unmoved mind where there is a perpetual Last Day, a trumpeting and coming up to judgment."[12]

The Achievement

Synge's achievement is one that is not local, however much his best art grew out of a strong sense of local life and his ability to render "the psychic state of the locality." His is an art rooted in the life he had known and in the people he had observed, but this fact does not make local art any more than it makes a folk art. It is the attitude of the artist, the comment that one chooses to make with one's material, that determines the level and focus of the art; and, although Synge sometimes takes a kind of primitivism for his medium, his total comment is never primitive, and he never accepts that limited view of the world that the folk artist by definition adopts.

Nor is Synge seen to best advantage as a "nature" writer, in spite of the attempts to so define his achievement, even by such an astute critic as Una Ellis-Fermor in *The Irish Dramatic Movement.* There is a strain of nature mysticism in Synge, as evidenced by some of the poems and by the persistent presence and treatment of nature in the plays; but Synge never offers, in his major work, nature for its own sake, as an end in itself. Nature is usually invoked for the contrast it provides to human society, for the comment the life of nature makes about the restrictive life of man in society. Synge had a deep feeling for nature and an equally strong awareness of nature's symbolic values to the artist for an expression of a total universe, but to label him as a nature writer is to limit him in the same way as those critics who would see him as a local writer or as a folk dramatist. Synge's ability to portray the conflicts between man's natural desires and the represssions of organized society has been translated by several critics into specifically Irish terms as the conflict between Oisin and St. Patrick: between a natural, pagan freedom and the highly organized restrictions of the church.[13] Nature and the natural life provided Synge with the images and vision for symbolizing the inevitable warfare between the two ways of life represented by Oisin and St. Patrick.

Synge's vision, a view of the world presented with consistency in *The Aran Islands* and in the plays, was one that makes his work particularly congenial to the modern reader. He insisted upon a realistic assessment of human life and the struggle that he felt it to be in the face of an alien universe and a vigorously beautiful but nonetheless indifferent nature. As Synge saw it, man's difficulties in such a universe were multiplied by his insistent attempt to impose his own rigid codes of behavior upon the world. This judgment is the source of the unique fusion in Synge's plays of the primitive world, the world of nature, and a social commentary that drama has ordinarily relegated to an urban, mechanized world. The primitive and the natural provide a meaningful structure for understanding the intensely basic nature of the conflicts and the lies that society has imposed upon itself.

Synge's attempt to revitalize the language of drama, to find a living idiom that could become a part of the dramatic experience, prefigured an unending concern of modern poetic dramatists. Although the solution he reached—a dramatic approximation of the vitality of peasant speech—is not realistically available to dramatists in all cultures,

Synge demonstrated what can be done when the language once again is set into operation as a total part of the dramatic whole. The use of rhetoric in *The Playboy* as a part of the whole statement of the play provides an example of the part language can play in fully realized drama.

The permanence of Synge's place in the world of drama is well assured by the inclusion of one of his plays (usually *Riders to the Sea* or *The Playboy of the Western World*) in every major anthology of modern drama. The persistence of his plays in production attests not only to their continued relevancy but also to their theatrical possibilities. Synge knew, in Yeats's words, "no voice but his own." It is a measure of Synge's accomplishment that his voice, speaking of the human condition, is one that is heard with clarity and meaning today.

Notes and References

Chapter One

1. W. B. Yeats, "To-morrow's Revolution," *Explorations* (London: Macmillan, 1962), 418.

2. W. B. Yeats, "Preface to the First Edition of *The Well of the Saints*," *Essays and Introductions* (London: Macmillan, 1961), 299.

3. Ibid., 298.

4. Alan Price, *Synge and Anglo-Irish Drama* (London: Methuen, 1961), 89.

5. W. B. Yeats, *A Vision* (New York: Macmillan, 1961), 167.

6. David H. Greene and Edward M. Stephens, *J. M. Synge, 1871–1909* (New York: Macmillan, 1959), 5.

7. An account of the family's version of the legend is given in the Reverend Samuel Synge's *Letters to My Daughter: Memories of John Millington Synge* (Dublin and Cork: Talbot Press, 1931), 8.

8. *In Wicklow, West Kerry and Connemara* (Dublin: Maunsel & Co., 1911), 1.

9. Ibid., 6.

10. Greene and Stephens, *Synge*, 71–72.

11. *The Aran Islands* (Boston: John W. Luce & Co., 1911), 166–67. All quotations from *The Aran Islands* are from this edition.

12. *E.g.*, P. P. Howe entitles his discussion of *The Aran Islands* "The Notebooks," in his *J. M. Synge: A Critical Study* (London: Secker, 1912). Corkery, while objecting to Howe's term, names his own chapter on *The Aran Islands* "The Essays," in his *Synge and Anglo-Irish Literature* (Cork: Cork University Press, 1931).

13. Mary C. King, *The Drama of J. M. Synge* (London: Fourth Estate, 1985), 20.

14. *Collected Works*, vol. 2, edited by Robin Skelton (London: Oxford University Press, 1966), 47.

15. Robin Skelton, *The Writings of J. M. Synge* (New York: Bobbs, Merrill, 1971), 39.

16. Flaherty's film gave rise in its turn to Gilbert Bécaud's *The Opera of Aran*, which premiered in Paris in 1962.

17. W. B. Yeats, "J. M. Synge and the Ireland of his Time," *Essays and Introductions*, 326.

18. Ibid., 325.

19. Greene and Stephens, *Synge*, 87.

Chapter Two

    1. Skelton, *Writings of J. M. Synge,* 18.
    2. From a memorandum to Synge's executors, Synge, *Collected Works,* 3:157.
    3. Saddlemyer's reconstructed text of the play in the Oxford edition of the *Collected Works* is a conflation of two one-act versions, the latest of which is used as the basic text.
    4. Ibid., 162.
    5. *My Uncle John: Edward Stephens's Life of J. M. Synge* (London: Oxford University Press, 1974), 147.

Chapter Three

    1. Lennox Robinson, *Ireland's Abbey Theatre: A History, 1899–1951* (London: Sidgwick & Jackson, 1951), 36.
    2. For a detailed study of the relationship between Synge and Ibsen, see Jan Setterquist, *Ibsen and the Beginnings of Anglo-Irish Drama. I: John Millington Synge* (Uppsala, Sweden: Uppsala University, 1951).
    3. Corkery, *Synge,* 125.
    4. Greene and Stephens, *Synge,* 157.
    5. A record is given by David H. Greene, *"The Shadow of the Glen* and *The Widow of Ephesus,"* PMLA, 62 (March 1947), 233–38.
    6. Corkery, *Synge,* 123.
    7. *The Complete Works of John M. Synge* (New York: Random House, 1935). All references to Synge's work, unless otherwise noted, are to this edition.
    8. *In Wicklow, West Kerry and Connemara,* 12.
    9. Declan Kiberd, *Synge and the Irish Language,* (Totowa, N.J.: Rowman & Littlefield, 1979), 168–74.
    10. Frank O'Connor, "Synge," in *The Irish Theatre,* ed. Lennox Robinson (London: Macmillan, 1939), 42.
    11. Ibid., 34.
    12. *The Autobiography of William Butler Yeats* (Garden City, N. Y.: Macmillan, 1938), 356.

Chapter Four

    1. Kiberd, *Synge and the Irish Language,* 163–68.
    2. Una Ellis-Fermor, *The Irish Dramatic Movement* (London: Methuen, 1954), 163.
    3. Mary C. King, *The Drama of J. M. Synge,* (London: Fourth Estate, 1985), 49.
    4. John Gassner, *The Theatre in Our Times* (New York: Random House, 1954), 3.

5. Greene and Stephens, *Synge,* 259.
6. Ibid., 157.

Chapter Five

1. W. G. Fay and Catherine Carswell, *The Fays of the Abbey Theatre* (New York: Harcourt, Brace, 1935), 168.
2. Greene and Stephens, *Synge,* 134–35.
3. Maurice Bourgeois, *John Millington Synge and the Irish Dramatic Movement* (London: Constable 1913), 220–21.
4. For the correspondence of Synge to Meyerfield, see *Yale Review* 13 (July 1924): 690–709.
5. O'Connor, "Synge," *The Irish Theatre,* 48–49.

Chapter Six

1. David Greene, "*The Tinker's Wedding*: A Revaluation," *PMLA* 62 (September 1947): 824–27.
2. Northrop Frye, *The Anatomy of Criticism* (Princeton: Princeton University Press, 1957), 163.
3. Ibid., 178.
4. See, for example, King and Skelton.
5. Frye, *Anatomy,* 169.
6. Ibid.
7. *Collected Works,* 4:291.
8. Yeats, *Essays and Introductions,* 87–88.
9. Greene and Stephens, *Synge,* 87–88.
10. Ibid., 182.
11. *Collected Works,* 2:149.

Chapter Seven

1. In "The *Playboy* and Irish Nationalism," *Journal of English and Germanic Philology* 46 (April 1947): 199–204. Greene discusses Synge's working drafts of the play.
2. Ellis-Fermor, *The Irish Dramatic Movement,* 179.
3. J. B. Yeats, "Synge and the Irish," *Essays Irish and American* (New York: Macmillan, 1918), 58.
4. Patricia M. Spacks has an interesting and illuminating discussion of this aspect of the play in her article, "The Making of the Playboy," in *Modern Drama* 4 (December 1961): 314–23.
5. See Irving Suss's comments in his essay, "The 'Playboy' Riots," *Irish Writing* 18 (March 1952): 39–42.
6. See Vivian Mercier, *The Irish Comic Tradition* (Oxford: Oxford University Press, 1962), 49–53.

7. Ibid., 239.

8. Ann Saddlemyer, *Letters to Molly* (Cambridge, Mass: Harvard University Press, 1971), 87–88.

9. Fay and Carswell, *Abbey Theatre,* 211.

10. Ibid., 212.

11. Ibid., 214.

12. Lady Gregory, *Our Irish Theatre* (London and New York: Putnam, 1913), 115.

13. Reprinted in Lady Gregory, *Our Irish Theatre,* 299.

14. Ibid., 301.

Chapter Eight

1. Greene and Stephens, *Synge,* 300.

2. Ibid., 156–57.

3. *Collected Works,* 4:370.

4. Ibid., 394.

5. Saddlemyer, *Letters to Molly,* 46.

6. *Collected Works,* 4:xxvi.

7. David Greene, "*The Tinker's Wedding,* A Revaluation," *PMLA* 62 (September 1947): 826.

8. Unpublished paper, "Pagan Symbolism in *Deirdre of the Sorrows*" by Arlene Hebert. In much of this discussion of Synge's use of such symbols I am indebted to Hebert for calling it to my attention.

9. Ibid.

10. William Empson, *Seven Types of Ambiguity* (New York: New Directions, 1955), 46–50.

11. W. B. Yeats, *Autobiography,* 330.

12. W. B. Yeats, *Essays and Introductions,* 238.

13. Ibid., 238–39.

Chapter Nine

1. "John M. Synge," reprinted in Masefield's *Recent Prose* (New York: Macmillan, 1933), 177.

2. For the text of "A Mountain Creed" and a discussion of Synge's early attempts at verse writing, see Greene and Stephens's biography.

3. Green and Stephens, *Synge,* 18–19.

4. Ibid., 11–13.

5. See, for example, Robin Skelton's article, "The Poetry of J. M. Synge," *Poetry Ireland* 1 (Autumn 1962):32–44.

6. Greene and Stephens, *Synge,* 127.

7. *Collected Works. Volume I: Poems,* ed. Robin Skelton (London: Oxford University Press, 1962), 69, 76.

8. Greene and Stephens, *Synge,* 113.

9. Ibid., 259.

10. Ibid., 113.

11. T. S. Eliot, "Poetry and Drama," *On Poetry and Poets* (New York: Farrar, Straus & Cudahy, 1957), 82.

12. Greene and Stephens, *Synge,* 84.

13. "Introduction," *J. M. Synge: Translations,* ed. Robin Skelton (Dublin: Dolmen Press, 1961), v.

14. A. G. Van Hamel, *Englische Studien,* Band 45 (1912):273.

15. "J. M. Synge," in L. A. G. Strong's *Personal Remarks* (New York: Haskell House, 1953), 44.

Chapter Ten

1. Recorded in "The Bounty of Sweden" in *Dramatis Personae* (New York: Macmillan, 1936).

2. Greene and Stephens, *Synge,* 269.

3. T. R. Henn, *The Lonely Tower* (London: Methuen, 1950), 105.

4. W. B. Yeats, *Explorations,* 442.

5. W. B. Yeats, *A Vision,* 165.

6. Proudly recorded by Lady Gregory in *Our Irish Theatre.*

7. Herbert Howarth, *The Irish Writers* (New York: Hill & Wang, 1959), 219.

8. See W. B. Yeats's poem, "Beautiful Lofty Things."

9. Howarth, *Irish Writers,* 240.

10. For an account of the relationship between Joyce and Synge, see Richard Ellmann, *James Joyce* (New York: Oxford University Press, 1959), 276.

11. Owen Quinn, "No Garland for John Synge," *Envoy* 3 (October 1950):51.

12. W. B. Yeats, *Essays and Introductions,* 310.

13. See, for example, David Krause, "'The Rageous Ossean': Patron-hero of Synge and O'Casey," *Modern Drama* 4 (December 1961):268–91.

Selected Bibliography

PRIMARY WORKS

Prose, First Editions

The Aran Islands, Dublin: Maunsel & Co.; London: Elkin Mathews, 1907. Frontispiece and illustrations by Jack B. Yeats. A few copies of this edition are dated 1906 and may have been advance copies. However, the first printing appeared in April 1907. One hundred and fifty copies were printed on large paper and signed by Jack Yeats and Synge.

The Autobiography of J. M. Synge. Edited by Alan Price with fourteen of Synge's photographs and an essay on Synge and the photography of his time by P. J. Pocock. Dublin: Dolmen Press, 1965.

The Works of John M. Synge. Vol. 4. Dublin: Maunsel & Co., 1910. The first printing of *In Wicklow* and *In West Kerry* in book form. Earlier versions had appeared as articles in the *Shanachie. In the Congested Districts* was originally printed in the *Manchester Guardian* and was not revised for the book printing.

Plays, First Editions

Riders to the Sea. In Samhain (Dublin, 1903), 25–33. A musical setting was composed and published by R. Vaughan Williams of *Riders to the Sea,* London: Oxford University Press; New York: Carl Fischer; Paris: Le Magasin Musical Pierre Schneider; Amsterdam: Brockmans & Van Poppel; Lausanne: Foetisch Freres S. A., 1937.

In the Shadow of the Glen. New York: John Quinn, 1904. Privately printed for American copyright purposes, this play is the first creative work of Synge's to be published separately. It appeared in the December 1904 *Samhain* with Lady Gregory's *Rising of the Moon.*

The Shadow of the Glen and Riders to the Sea. London: Elkin Mathews, 1905. This edition constitutes the first commercial publication in book form of Synge's work.

The Well of the Saints. London: A. H. Bullen, 1905. Vol. 1 of the Abbey Theatre Series, this small edition was published for sale in the Abbey Theatre when the play opened there on 3 February 1905. A more expensive edition, containing a preface by W. B. Yeats, was printed later in the year by A. H. Bullen as vol. 4 of the Plays for an Irish Theatre Series.

John Quinn published an edition limited to fifty copies in New York in
1905.

The Playboy of the Western World. Dublin: Maunsel & Co., 1907. As vol. 10 of
the Abbey Theatre Series, this play was printed in a limited number of
copies prior to the first production of the play at the Abbey Theatre, 26
January 1907. An edition with a preface by Synge was published by
Maunsel & Co. later in 1907. In order to preserve the copyright, John
Quinn published twelve copies of act 2 in New York in 1907.

The Tinker's Wedding. Dublin: Maunsel & Co., 1908.

Deirdre of the Sorrows. Dundrum: Cuala Press, 1910. John Quinn printed fifty
copies in New York in 1910, from the proof sheets of the Cuala Press
edition. According to the Quinn sale catalog of 1924, because of excessive
errors all but five copies on vellum and five copies on handmade paper
were destroyed.

Poems and Translations, First Editions

Poems and Translations. Dundrum: Cuala Press, 1909. This edition has a long
preface by W. B. Yeats. Fifty copies, including the preface by Yeats, were
printed by John Quinn in New York in 1909.

Essays and Reviews

"A Story from Inishmaan." *New Ireland Review* 10 (Dublin, November
1898):153–56.

"*La Sagesse et la Destinée.*" *Daily Express* (Dublin, December 1898), 3. A short
review of *La Sagesse et la Destinée* by Maurice Maeterlinck.

"Anatole Le Braz: A Breton Writer." *Daily Express* (Dublin, January 1899), 3.

"A Celtic Theatre." *Freeman's Journal* (Dublin, March 1900), 4.

"The Poems of Geoffrey Keating." *Speaker* (London, December 1900), 245. A
review of Father J. C. MacErlean's edition of Keating's poetry.

"The Last Fortress of the Celt." *Gael* (New York, April 1901), 109.

"*La Vieille Littérature Irlandaise.*" *L'Européen* (Paris, March 1902), 11.

"*Le Mouvement Intellectual Irlandais.*" *L'Européen* (Paris, May 1902), 12.

"An Epic of Ulster." *Speaker* (London, June 1902), 284–85. A review of *Cuchulain of Muirthemne,* by Lady Augusta Gregory.

"Irish Fairy Stories." *Speaker* (London, June 1902), 340. A review of *Donegal
Fairy Stories,* by Seumas MacManus.

"An Irish Historian." *Speaker* (London, September 1902), 605–6. A review of
David Comyn's edition of *The History of Ireland,* by Geoffrey Keating.

"The Old and New in Ireland." *Academy and Literature* (London, September
1902), 238–39.

"A Dream on Inishmaan." *Green Sheaf,* no. 2 (London, 1903):8–9.

"Loti and Huysmans." *Speaker* (London, April 1903), 57–58. A comparative review of *L'Inde sans les Anglais*, by Pierre Loti; *L'Oblat*, by J. K. Huysmans; and *Monsieur Bergeret à Paris*, by Anatole France.

"An Autumn Night in the Hills." *Gael* (New York, April 1903), 117.

"Celtic Mythology." *Speaker* (London, April 1904), 17–18. Review of R. I. Best's translation of *The Irish Mythological Cycle and Celtic Mythology*, by H. D'Arbois de Jubainville.

"The Winged Destiny." *Academy and Literature* (London, November 1904), 455. Short review of *The Winged Destiny*, by Fiona Macleod.

"An Impression of Aran." *Manchester Guardian*, 24 January 1905, 12.

"Letter concerning *In the Shadow of the Glen*." *United Irishman* (Dublin, 11 February 1905), 1.

"The Oppression of the Hills." *Manchester Guardian*, 15 February 1905, 12.

"In the Congested Districts." *Manchester Guardian* (June through July 1905). Illustrated by Jack B. Yeats.

"A Translation of Irish Romance." *Manchester Guardian*, 6 March 1906, 5. Review of *Heroic Romances of Ireland*, by A. H. Leahy.

"The Vagrants of Wicklow." *Shanachie*, no. 2 (Dublin, Autumn 1906):93–98.

"The Fair Hills of Ireland." *Manchester Guardian*, 16 November 1906, 5. Review of *The Fair Hills of Ireland*, by Stephen Gwynn.

"Letter concerning *The Playboy of the Western World*." *Irish Times*, 31 January 1907.

"The People of the Glens." *Shanachie*, no. 3 (Dublin, Spring 1907):39–47.

"At a Wicklow Fair: The Place and the People." *Manchester Guardian*, 9 May 1907, 12.

"In West Kerry." *Shanachie*, no. 4 (Dublin, Summer 1907):61–70.

"A Landlord's Garden: In County Wicklow." *Manchester Guardian*, 1 July 1907, 12.

"In West Kerry: The Blasket Islands." *Shanachie*, no. 5 (Dublin, Autumn 1907):138–50.

"In West Kerry: To Puck Fair." *Shanachie*, no. 6 (Dublin, Winter 1907):233–43.

"Good Pictures in Dublin: The New Municipal Gallery." *Manchester Guardian*, 24 January 1908, 12.

"In Wicklow: On the Road." *Manchester Guardian*, 10 December 1908, 14.

Principal Collected Editions

The Works of John M. Synge. 4 vols. Dublin: Maunsel & Co., 1910. Separate pocket and library editions of individual works were issued by Maunsel in the two years following.

Separate printings of all the plays and *The Aran Islands*. Boston: John W. Luce & Co., 1911.

The Works of John M. Synge. 4 vols. Boston: John W. Luce & Co., 1912.

The Dramatic Works of John M. Synge. Dublin and London: Maunsel & Co., 1915. The first one-volume edition of the plays.

Plays. London: George Allen & Unwin, 1924. Reprinted in 1929. In 1932 Unwin published a revised collected edition, *Plays,* by John M. Synge, which contains a revision of the third act of *The Well of the Saints,* a previously unpublished letter by Synge, and extracts from his notebooks. The revised edition appeared again in 1938 under the title of: *The Works of John M. Synge, Vol. 1—Plays.* In 1949 it was reprinted under the original title *Plays,* by John M. Synge.

Poems and Translations. London: George Allen & Unwin, 1924.

Plays. Revised collected edition. London: George Allen & Unwin, 1932. The revised version of act 3 of *The Well of the Saints* appears in this edition. A previously unpublished Synge letter and extracts from his notebooks are included in the volume.

The Aran Islands. London: George Allen & Unwin, 1934. Apparently reprinted from the Maunsel & Co., 1911, plates.

Plays by John M. Synge: The Playboy of the Western World, The Tinker's Wedding, The Shadow of the Glen. Guild Books no. 217. London: George Allen & Unwin, 1941.

Plays by John M. Synge: Riders to the Sea, Deirdre of the Sorrows, The Well of the Saints. Guild Books no. 218. London: George Allen & Unwin, 1941. Act 3 of *The Well of the Saints* is the revised version of the text.

The Complete Works of John M. Synge. New York: Random House, 1935.

John M. Synge: Collected Plays. Harmondsworth, Middlesex: Penguin Books, 1952. The text of act 3 of *The Well of the Saints* is the revised version.

John M. Synge: Plays, Poems and Prose. London: J. M. Dent & Sons, 1941. An introduction by Ernest Rhys appears in this volume. Act 3 of *The Well of the Saints* is the unrevised version of the text. Under the Everyman format, a reprint was made in 1958 with an introduction by Michael MacLiammoir.

Synge: Collected Works. Edited by Robin Skelton. London: Oxford University Press, 1962–68. The definitive edition that provides material from Synge's working papers.

Recordings

Riders to the Sea and In the Shadow of the Glen. Spoken Arts recording, 743. Radio Eireann Players' Production.

The Playboy of the Western World. Angel recordings 35357 and 35358. With Siobhan McKenna and Cyril Cusack.

Letters

"Letters of John Millington Synge: From Material Supplied by Max Meyerfield." *Yale Review* 13 (July 1924):690–709.

Letters to Molly: John Millington Synge to Maire O'Neill, 1906–1909. Edited by
Ann Saddlemyer. Cambridge, Mass.: Harvard University Press, 1971.

SECONDARY WORKS

Books

Bourgeois, Maurice. *John Millington Synge and the Irish Dramatic Movement.*
London: Constable, 1913. Best of the early works on Synge.

Bushrui, S. B., ed. *Sunshine and the Moon's Delight: A Centenary Tribute to
J. M. Synge.* Gerrards Cross: Colin Smythe, 1979. A collection of wide-
ranging essays by major critics of Synge. Of particular interest is a selection of essays dealing with Synge's reception in non-English-speaking
countries.

Clark, David. R., ed. *John Millington Synge: "Riders to the Sea."* Columbus:
Ohio State University Press, 1970. Useful collection of essays on the play.

Corkery, Daniel. *Synge and Anglo-Irish Literature.* 1931; Dublin and Cork:
Cork University Press, 1947. Of limited interest because Corkery's attempt to place Synge in terms of his "Anglo-Irish" heritage obscures and
prejudices the issues.

Coxhead, Elizabeth. *J. M. Synge and Lady Gregory.* Writers and Their Work,
no. 149. London: Longmans, Green, 1962. A British Book Council and
National Book League pamphlet. Brief, general, but useful study of
Synge and Lady Gregory.

Deane, Seamus. *Celtic Revivals.* London: Faber & Faber, 1985. Chapter on
Synge sees in his work a sense of the passing of Irish heritage and ideas
of heroism.

Ellis-Fermor, Una. *The Irish Dramatic Movement.* 2d. ed., rev. London: Methuen, 1954. Most reliable history of the Irish movement, with a chapter
devoted to Synge.

Fay, Gerard. *The Abbey Theatre: Cradle of Genius.* Dublin: Clonmore & Rey-
nolds, 1958. General survey of the work of the Abbey Theatre.

Fay, W. G., and Catherine Carswell. *The Fays of the Abbey Theatre: An
Autobiographical Record.* New York: Harcourt Brace, 1935. Interesting
and useful, if not always accurate.

Greene, David H., and Edward M. Stephens. *J. M. Synge, 1871–1909.*
New York: Macmillan, 1959, 1961. The official biography, which contains material from the Synge papers not elsewhere available; easily the
most valuable work on Synge.

Gregory, Lady Augusta. *Our Irish Theatre.* New York: Putnam, 1913. Lady

Gregory's recollections of the beginnings and significant years of the Abbey Theatre. The *Playboy* riots are given special treatment, and appendices provide reprints of some of the materials of the controversy.

Grene, Nicholas. *Synge.* Totowa, N. J.: Rowman & Littlefield, 1975. Readings of the plays.

Henn, Thomas Rice. *The Lonely Tower: Studies in the Poetry of W. B. Yeats.* London: Methuen, 1950. Chapter on Yeats and Synge provides a good appraisal of the relationship between the two contemporaries.

Howarth, Herbert. *The Irish Writers: Literature and Nationalism, 1880–1940.* New York: Hill & Wang, 1959. Surveys the principal Irish writers, with the chapter on Synge serving a special function as a corrective to attempts to romanticize Synge and his work. Also of interest for the account of Joyce's debt to Synge.

Kiberd, Declan. *Synge and the Irish Language.* Totowa, N. J.: Rowman & Littlefield, 1979. A major study of Synge and his Irish influences.

King, Mary C. *The Drama of J. M. Synge.* London: Fourth Estate, 1985. Thoughtful reading of Synge's work with a vaguely Marxist interest.

Masefield, John. *John M. Synge: A Few Personal Recollections with Biographical Notes.* Churchtown, Dundrum: Cuala Press, 1915. Reprinted in Masefield, *Recent Prose.* London: Macmillan, 1924. Interesting, but not always accurate memories of Synge and his career.

Moore, George. *Hail and Farewell.* Vol. 3. London: Heinemann, 1920. Of particular interest is Moore's account of Yeats's first meeting with Synge *after* Synge had been to the Aran Islands.

O'Connor, Frank. "Synge." In *The Irish Theatre: Lectures Delivered During the Abbey Theatre Festival Held in Dublin in August 1938,* edited by Lennox Robinson. London: Macmillan, 1939. Excellent estimation of the weakness in Daniel Corkery's approach to Synge and of Synge's unrecognized strengths.

O Síocháin, P. A. *Aran: Islands of Legend.* Dublin: Foilsiúcháin Eireann, 1962. Detailed account of the geography and history of the Aran Islands; several chapters discuss Synge's visits to the islands.

Peacock, Ronald. *The Poet in the Theatre.* New York: Hill & Wang, 1946, 1960. A view of Synge as a nineteenth-century, romantic sensibility. In general, a dissenting opinion.

Price, Alan. *Synge and Anglo-Irish Drama.* London: Methuen, 1961. Like Yeats in his preface to *The Well of the Saints,* Price finds Synge's major theme to be the conflict between dream and reality and examines Synge's work on this basis; the result is often perceptive study.

Robinson, Lennox. *Ireland's Abbey Theatre: A History, 1899–1951.* London: Sidgwick & Jackson, 1951. Detailed account and record of much useful material.

Saddlemyer, Ann. *J. M. Synge and Modern Comedy.* Dublin: Dolmen Press, 1965. Study examines Synge's ideas of comedy and his accomplishment.

Setterquist, Jan. *Ibsen and the Beginnings of Anglo-Irish Drama. I: John Mil-*
lington Synge. Uppsala Irish Studies, no. 2. Uppsala, Sweden: Uppsala
University, 1951. A study based on the assumption that in spite of his
asserted dislike for Ibsen, Synge was much influenced by Ibsen and that
there are many parallels in the works of the two playwrights—proof of
which is often forced and distorted to make a particular case.

Skelton, Robin. *The Writings of J. M. Synge.* New York: Bobbs Merrill, 1971.
A general assessment of all of Synge's works.

Thornton, Weldon. *J. M. Synge and the Western Mind.* Gerrards Cross, Bucks:
Colin Smythe, 1979. A study that assesses Synge within the Western,
specifically, religious tradition.

Yeats, John Butler. *Essays Irish and American.* New York: Macmillan, 1918.
A perceptive and important evaluation by the poet's father.

Yeats, W. B. *The Cutting of an Agate.* New York: Macmillan, 1912. Also in
Essays (London: Macmillan, 1924) and *Essays and Introductions* (London:
Macmillan, 1961). Contains Yeats's prefaces to the first editions of *The
Well of the Saints* and of *Poems and Translations* and the essay "J. M. Synge
and the Ireland of his Time," published separately by the Cuala Press
(Churchtown, Dundrum, 1911).

————. *The Death of Synge.* Dublin: Cuala Press, 1928. Also in *Dramatis
Personae* (New York: Macmillan, 1936) and *The Autobiography of William
Butler Yeats* (New York: Macmillan, 1938).

————. *The Irish Dramatic Movement.* In *Plays and Controversies* (London: Macmillan, 1923) and *Explorations* (London: Macmillan, 1962). The best
source for Yeats's interpretation of the meaning of the Irish Theatre movement and its events. Includes his essays on *Playboy* troubles.

Articles

Ayling, Ronald, F. "Synge's First Love: Some South African Aspects." *Modern
Drama* 6 (February 1964):450–60. Recollections of Synge by Cherrie
Matheson.

Barnes, T. R. "Yeats, Synge, Ibsen and Strindberg." *Scrutiny* 5 (December
1936):257–62.

Cusack, Cyril. "A Player's Reflections on *Playboy.*" *Modern Drama* 4 (December 1961):300–305. Comments by one of the Abbey players.

Davie, Donald. "The Poetic Diction of Synge." *Dublin Magazine* 27, n. s.
(January–March 1952):32–38. First serious attempt to examine Synge as
a poet.

Donoghue, Denis. "Synge: *Riders to the Sea*; a Study." *University Review* 1
(Summer 1955):52–58. Examines the symbolism of the play.

————. "'Too Immoral for Dublin': Synge's *The Tinker's Wedding.*" *Irish Writing* 30 (March 1955):56–62. Survey of reasons *The Tinker's Wedding* could
not be staged.

Gerstenberger, Donna. "Bonnie and Clyde and Christy Mahon: Playboys All." *Modern Drama* 14 (1971). A consideration of the use of similar comic effects in Synge's play and Arthur Penn's movie.

Greene, David H. "The *Playboy* and Irish Nationalism." *Journal of English and Germanic Philology* 46 (April 1947):199–204. Good discussion of Synge's working drafts of *Playboy.*

————. "*The Shadow of the Glen* and *The Widow of Ephesus.*" PMLA 62 (March 1947):233–38. Study of Synge's sources for his play.

————. "Synge and the Celtic Revival." *Modern Drama* 4 (December 1961):292–99. Evaluation of Synge's general relationship to the revival of Irish national concerns.

————. "Synge's Unfinished *Deirdre.*" PMLA 63 (December 1948), 1314–21. Surveys the *Deirdre* manuscripts.

————. "*The Tinker's Wedding,* a Revaluation." PMLA 62 (September 1947):824–27. Useful examination of Synge's changes in versions of the play.

Krause, David. "'The Rageous Ossean': Patron-Hero of Synge and O'Casey," *Modern Drama* 4 (December 1961):268–91. A discussion of the implications of the Christian attempts to tame the mythic Irish hero, a conflict with special meaning for Synge and O'Casey.

Levitt, Paul. "The Structural Craftsmanship of J. M. Synge's *Riders to the Sea.*" *Eire-Ireland* 4 (1969). Useful examination of the play.

Leyburn, Ellen Douglas. "The Theme of Loneliness in the Plays of Synge." *Modern Drama* (September 1958):84–90.

Maclean, Hugh H. "The Hero as Playboy." *University of Kansas City Review* 21 (Autumn 1954):9–19. This discussion centers on a reading of the play as scapegoat myth, with Christy (n.b. his name) as a kind of Christ: a suggestive but often forced reading of the play (Pegeen denies Christy *three* times, etc).

Mercer, Caroline G. "Stephen Dedalus' Vision and Synge's Peasant Girls." *Notes and Queries* 7 (December 1960):473–74. Joyce's wading girl in *Portrait of the Artist* is compared to a similar scene in *The Aran Islands,* which is considered as Joyce's source, a suggestion earlier made by Herbert Howarth in *The Irish Writers.*

Murphy, Daniel J. "The Reception of Synge's *Playboy* in Ireland and America: 1907–1912." *Bulletin of the New York Public Library* 64 (October 1960):515–33. A good record of the reactions to the play.

O'Neill, Michael J. "Holloway on Synge's Last Days." *Modern Drama* 6 (September 1963):126–30. Since Holloway was unable to understand Synge, his comments on Synge's death need to be read with care.

Orel, Harold. "Synge's Last Play: 'And a Story Will be Told For Ever.'" *Modern Drama* 4 (December 1961):306–13. Examination of Synge's unfinished *Deirdre of the Sorrows.*

Podhoretz, Norman. "Synge's *Playboy*: Morality and the Hero." *Essays in*

Criticism 3 (July 1953):337–44. Examines moral implication of Christy's transformation.

Price, Alan F. "A Consideration of Synge's *The Shadow of the Glen.*" *Dublin Magazine* 26 (October–December 1951):15–24. An essay reprinted as part of Price's *Synge and Anglo-Irish Drama.*

Quinn, Owen. "No Garland for John Synge." *Envoy* 3 (October 1950):44–51. Asserts that Synge was "totally unfitted for the task of collaborating with Irish Catholic life, rustic or otherwise," and that he only portrays the world of the imagination. Contains the sentence that Synge's work "is unlikely to have any bearing, except in a negative way, on the future of [Irish] literature."

Skelton, Robin. "The Poetry of J. M. Synge." *Poetry Ireland* 1 (Autumn 1962):32–44. Serious study of the poetry.

Spacks, Patricia Meyer. "The Making of the Playboy." *Modern Drama* 4 (December 1961):314–23. Interesting, provocative reading of *The Playboy of the Western World* as folk myth.

Suss, Irving D. "The *Playboy* Riots." *Irish Writing* 18 (March 1952):39–42. Suggests that the political causes of the riots should not overshadow the deep-lying social causes.

Van Hamel, A. G. "On Anglo-Irish Syntax." *Englische Studien,* Band 45 (1912):272–92. Early but still useful study of the syntax of Anglo-Irish speech.

Bibliography

Levitt, Paul. *J. M. Synge: A Bibliography of Published Criticism.* Dublin: Dolmen Press, 1974.

Index